By the same author

Juvenile Violence in a Winner–Loser Culture (1995)

Britain on the Couch: How Keeping Up with the Joneses Has Depressed Us since 1950 (1997)

They F*** You Up: How to Survive Family Life (2002)

Affluenza: How to Be Successful and Stay Sane (2007)

The Selfish Capitalist: Origins of Affluenza (2008)

Contented Dementia: 24-Hour Wraparound Care for Lifelong Well-being (2009)

How Not to F*** Them Up (2010)

Love Bombing

Reset your child's emotional thermostat

Oliver James

KARNAC

First published in 2012 by
Karnac Books
118 Finchley Road
London NW3 5HT

British Library Cataloguing in Publication Data

A C.I.P. card for this book is available from the British Library

ISBN: 978-1-78049-137-0

Edited, designed, and produced by Communication Crafts

Printed in Great Britain

www.karnacbooks.com

To Jean Knox,
and to all the children and parents whose brains
and relationships may benefit from this technique

CONTENTS

Acknowledgements   ix

The stories   xi

One   All about Love Bombing   1

Two   Temper tantrums, defiance, raging   25

Three   Anxiousness, nerviness, shyness   53

Four   Self-loathing, wanting to die   72

Five   Sleep problems   85

Six   Hyperactivity   93

Seven   Perfectionism   115

Eight   Autism   125

Nine   Love Bombing in shorter bursts   155

Ten   When Love Bombing didn't work   177

Further reading   223

ACKNOWLEDGEMENTS

Many thanks to Oliver Rathbone of Karnac Books for taking this project on and backing it to the hilt. Also at Karnac, to Alex Massey for his hard work in marketing it. Thanks to Jo Jacobius for enthusiastic, engaged publicizing.

Thanks to Shu Richmond at ITV's *This Morning* programme for giving me the chance to make the programmes that led to the method.

A big thankyou to Patrick Neale of Jaffé & Neale bookshop in Chipping Norton. He provided me with useful contacts, but even more important gave me faith that this project could work.

Thanks to the numerous retailers of books who have been good enough to stock this one. At WH Smith, Karen West was kind enough not only to hear our pitch, but to offer useful advice. At Waterstones, Peter Saxton offered me helpful suggestions and contacts. Thanks to Philip Blackwell for getting behind the project. Thanks to Rosalind Bridges at Amazon for her words of wisdom.

As ever, thanks to my wife Clare for her unstinting support as I disappeared off chasing my deadline, and to Olive and Louis, my children, for putting up with sporadic unavailability.

Most of all, a big thankyou to all the parents who were good enough to share their experiences of Love Bombing with me. They must necessarily remain anonymous, but in being so detailed and taking the trouble to communicate what it was like, they have made this book possible: thank you.

THE STORIES

Parents' experiences of Love Bombing

STORY 1   Two nights away – single mother   27
A son who replicates his father's anger attacks:
Sean, aged 12

STORY 2   Two nights away   37
Hostile rejection of mother: Tanya, aged 4

STORY 3   One night away   44
Short-fused son, fussy mother likes clear rules:
Todd, aged 6

STORY 4   Two awaydays   54
Fear of separation from mother: Sam, aged 3

STORY 5   One night away   66
Scared of groups, scared of losing toys: Gina, aged 3

STORY 6   Two nights away   73
Self-loathing, meltdowns: Tim, aged 9

STORY 7   One night away   86
Waking 25 times a night: Jess, aged 8

STORY 8   One night away – single mother   94
Hyperactive and violent: Kim, aged 7

STORY 9   One awayday   104
Hyperactive, insecure identical twins:
Claire and Loki, aged 4½

STORY 10   24 hours at home – single mother   116
Perfectionism, mild OCD, locked down emotionally:
Mark, aged 11

STORY 11   Five weekends of two nights away   126
Autistic, prone to meltdowns: Sara, aged 8

STORY 12   Morning half-hours   156
Defiance: Dawn, aged 9

STORY 13   An hour or two of LB, several times a week   162
Temper tantrums: Mick, aged 8

STORY 14   Two hours, fortnightly   164
Sibling rivalry: Seamus, aged 3
Estrangement from mother: Paddy, aged 7

STORY 15   LB as part of everyday life   167
Neediness and truculence: Greta, aged 3

STORY 16   LB play sessions   168
Easily distressed: Jeff, aged 4

STORY 17   Two nights away   178
Talented, rebelling against school and underachieving:
John, aged 13

STORY 18   Two nights away   190
Made nervy and angry by parents rowing: Mary, aged 10

STORY 19   An awayday – single father   213
Self-loathing, tantrums, overeating: Sheila, aged 11

STORY 20   One night away   216
A dyspraxic, self-hating and meltdown-prone identical twin:
Tina, aged 7

Love Bombing

ONE

All about Love Bombing

WHAT IS LOVE BOMBING?

Perhaps your child is a bit troubled in just one respect, like a little shy or sometimes over-demanding. Maybe he or she has much more numerous and serious problems, like severe temper tantrums at the age of 10, or being paralysed by groundless fears. Either way, Love Bombing can help.

The child's problem is almost never the fault of parents, who are only doing their best. Because of one misfortune or another, or a chain of them, the child's basic brain chemistry is in need of adjustment, usually only a small one. Perhaps surprisingly, rather than a pill being the best way to achieve this, it is far more effective to give the child a new experience and to alter the way the parents relate to him or her.

One of the most astonishing and significant scientific discoveries of the last ten years is that children's brains are much more plastic – malleable – than previously believed. We have an emotional thermostat, and luckily it *is* a thermostat. Just as you can alter the amount of heating or air-conditioning in your home, so you can adjust your child's brain. Of course, making the change takes more effort than just turning a dial, which is where Love Bombing comes in: you do not have to agonize about what went wrong in the past or beat yourself up about that stuff – the joy of Love Bombing is you can just get on with putting things right.

Love Bombing gives your child a very intense, condensed experience of feeling completely loved and completely in control. The period during which this is done can be 48 hours (two nights), 24 hours (one night), a single day, or shorter bursts. Whichever period you use, you subsequently rekindle that experience daily for half an hour. Dramatic shifts result in the child's personality and behaviour. When it comes to dealing with disobedient or shy or clingy or aggressive or impatient children, love and control, it seems, really are the answer. What is more, because so many parents are, or have had periods of, living very busy or miserable or complicated lives, most of us need to reconnect with our children from time to time. Love Bombing does the job.

The method works equally well whatever your social background, ethnic origin or nationality: the fundamental needs of children are the same everywhere. It can be done with no financial cost. It works for nearly all children from the age of 3 years to the early teens.

Originally, I developed the method when making three parenting series for British television (ITV's *This Morning*). The producers told me they would take me to the home of a child whose parents were worried about their child. I was to provide the parents with The Answer – and two weeks later we would return to find that the problem had been solved!

I admit that I was sceptical that this would be possible with the angry and defiant children they had lined up for me, often from harassed low-income homes. By good fortune, I happened to read a scientific paper at that time which described a much more intense version of the method I eventually developed and which, somewhat to my surprise, worked remarkably well for a very wide variety of difficulties. Over one hundred parents have now followed my method.

In this chapter, I describe what is involved and address some queries you may have about the method. In the rest of the book, I present twenty stories of parents who have done it, with the chapters organized according to the problems their children had. All these parents were sent a basic four-page plan, or protocol, for how to do Love Bombing, very similar in content to this chapter.

After reading this chapter, I suggest that you start by going to the chapter that relates to the kind of problem that is closest to the one your child may have. After that, as explained in the section below answering 'Frequently Asked Questions', I suggest you move around the book looking at stories that relate to different ways of doing Love Bombing, such as for two nights, one night, or an awayday. If you are short of money or do not want any expense, you may want to read examples where there is very little cost or none. You may also want to know about doing it with children of a similar age to yours, albeit that their problems might be different. If you are a single parent, you can find stories by other parents in the same position as you. You may be very short of time, in which case there is a whole chapter (Chapter Nine) devoted to brief ways of doing Love Bombing. There are also two stories involving identical twins, if you have them. If you are curious what might prevent Love Bombing working, read the stories in Chapter Ten.

For simplicity, in general cases I will refer the child to as a boy – even though, of course, problems are by no means limited to boys!

HOW TO LOVE BOMB

Love Bombing (henceforth I will just use the initials LB to indicate the words) is spending a period of time alone with your child, offering him a lot of love and giving him control. This is not the same thing as 'quality time', where you just hang out with your child. When you Love Bomb, you create a special emotional zone that your child and you regard as wholly different from your normal life, with new rules.

You may be thinking, 'Are you mad? My child is already a tyrant – rewarding him with love and giving him total control is just going to make it even worse!' That would be an understandable response: LB seems to fly in the face of the accepted wisdom, which often recommends more control, not less, and stricter, firmer reactions to undesirable behaviour. But remember, the LB zone is separate from ordinary life. I am not suggesting that once out of that zone you give up trying to set boundaries. In fact, the LB experience will feed back into your normal life in a very benign way, greatly reducing the amount of time you spend imposing limits, nagging and nattering – the 'Don't do that', 'I've told you before, put that down', 'Leave your sister alone', into which all parents get sucked sometimes.

A key practical decision you need to make at the outset is the length of time you will spend in the LB zone and the frequency. At one extreme, you can take your child away from the family home for a couple of nights. If you can afford it, you might go to a hotel or bed & breakfast (or rent a cheap gypsy caravan, as one mother did). Alternatively, as many parents have done, the rest of your family can spend the weekend with relatives or friends, leaving you at home with your child. If you feel it is important to get away from your normal environment, your home, you may be able persuade a relative or friend to swap homes for a night. There is absolutely no necessity to spend any extra money to do LB, although some of the stories in the book entail parents using money to make it easier for themselves, or because they felt that was a good way to help create the zone of love and control.

The simplest way to explain to you what the key elements in LB are is to describe what happens if you spend two nights and days exclusively alone with your child, whether at home or somewhere else. Before describing this, though, remember that it is very much not the only way or necessarily the best way for you: in the chapters that follow there are accounts of parents who did LB for just half an hour a day at home, or spent three hours of a day every fortnight going to the park. In reading what follows, if you are thinking 'I could never afford to do this' or 'this would be totally impractical, who would look after my other children?', remember that there are plenty of alternatives to two nights and days alone.

What is more, there is no rigid 'Best Way' once you enter the LB zone. I do suggest a basic plan, or protocol, but in most cases parents customize it to suit their particular practical circumstances and their child. In reading what follows, therefore, do not feel there are any strict rules that have to be followed: look upon it as a broad outline that you are going to colonize and make your own – just as your child will.

Two nights away

1. Explaining it to the child

The idea is very, very simple: you are going to give your child 48 hours of feeling in Total Control and having Unconditional Love.

First, you explain to your child that sometime soon, the two of you are going to spend a weekend together and are going to have a lot of fun. He is going to decide what he wants and when he wants it, within reason: you give the message that this is going to be a Big Event, It's Coming Soon – How Exciting!

At least one week beforehand, you ask your child 'What are the things that you most want to do in the world?' You tell him you will do your best to arrange for that to happen. You build up to the event by saying, 'We are going to have Total Time together – let's make a plan of all the things you would really, really like to do.' He then draws up a list. It doesn't matter if that includes lots of watching *Spongebob Squarepants* or suchlike: the key is that it is your child who has chosen it. During the experience, you are trying, as much as possible, to give him the feeling that 'whatever I want, I get' – a very unusual experience of being in control and of being gratified.

Obviously, this has to be within reason. Where you hit limits (often financial, sometimes practical), you have to be crafty. A demand to continuously eat hyperactivity-inducing quantities of sweets containing additives may be side-stepped by finding ones that are free of them. Going to the moon in a rocket needs similar side-stepping, but oddly enough, in the vast majority of cases, the child will accept this once he has realized how exciting and different from normal it is going to be. None of the parents who have done LB actually found it difficult to accommodate what their children wanted: what your child really wants is you.

It is important that you ask your child to think of a name to give the experience, whether that's Special Time or something more eccentric – it does not matter. You do not have to settle this right away, and your child can change the name, but the crucial thing is that it comes from the child, not the parent. He may have a shorthand title for it beforehand which alters during the experience. The important thing is that afterwards this label will instantly recall it.

2. LB during the time away

As often as possible, you will tell your child that you love him, as much as possible really meaning it (alas, there may be times when the child is unlovable . . .). You need to try from time to time to sit the child down and look him in the eye when telling him, though this will not always be feasible. It might seem a bit unnatural and weird at first, but he will get the idea if you just keep plugging away. Alongside this, you will hug him a great deal, tell him reassuring things like that everything is alright, there is nothing to worry about today or at home, he is completely safe with you. In doing this, you are distilling an experience of what it was like to bask in feeling loved and looked after, safely and reliably, when much smaller.

In most cases, parents share their bed with their child during the LB. This gives the child a strong feeling of intimacy and safety, helping to encourage him to relax and feel like a small child again.

Whatever the child's actual age, it can help to think of him as an 18-month-old for much of the LB period. Regardless of age, parents have reported to me that their child has brief periods during the LB when he actually reverts to being like a toddler, cuddling and even using baby talk. This is exactly what you are aiming for. You are trying to give him the chance to go back to earlier periods, but this time it is really, really good: he feels totally safe, loved and in control.

3. Why this helps

Allowing your child to choose what is done gives him a strong sense of getting his needs met when, either today or earlier in life, he may have felt this was erratic and he could never be sure that what he wanted – control – would happen. Equally, by pouring love over your child, you are making him feel of tremendous importance to you, able to bathe in the affection that – through no fault of yours – may now or in the past have been missing at times.

What this does is to reset the key brain chemicals, especially cortisol, the fight–flight hormone secreted when we feel fearful. If a child has constantly high levels of cortisol, or is too easily provoked to rack them up by events that are actually not threatening, he is jammed in a state of fear, expecting something to go wrong. That is the root cause of so much of the aggression or hyperactivity or anxiety that plagues so many of our children. By giving them a feeling of total security, that there's nothing to worry about, you make them feel loved, valued and in control, as opposed to a dangerous situation in which at any moment things could go pear-shaped. Even short periods of feeling like that seem, surprisingly, to rebalance the cortisol levels, enabling the child to regulate himself rather than lose control.

Most parents report that, oddly enough, the experience also seems to reset their own thermostat in relation to the child. The difficult behaviour of our children means that nearly all of us find ourselves sucked into shouting, getting red-faced, becoming fairly childish ourselves. This can become a habit. LB seems to reset the parental parenting thermostat, as well as the child's.

4. Troubleshooting

There will probably be times when you find it hard to deal with your child during the two days of LB. He could try to wind you up, because there will be anger there, alongside the fearfulness and sadness. He may also try to push the boundaries to see how real your love is. There may be tantrums. You are encouraging him to become like a toddler, so that is not surprising.

In many respects, it's best to react to this as you would to an 18-month-old. Keeping emotions under control is difficult at that age, and in all likelihood the problem is that he has not managed to make some key advance in his development. Although now aged 5 or 10, your child may not have learnt to press the 'pause' button when frustrated, may be prone to being swamped with emotion and behaving childishly. If tantrums do happen during the LB, that may be positive as long as you can stay calm and show him it's fine, you are still there, your love can withstand the assaults. This enables your child to be detached rather than succumbing to emotional meltdown: the detachment is the 'pause' button.

This may sound completely counter-intuitive, like a recipe for creating a spoilt brat, especially if your child seems never to feel he has enough. Surely such 'giving in' will only teach him to be even more demanding? So many books and TV programmes suggest that where disobedient or aggressive behaviour are the problem, what is needed are 'Naughty Steps', 'Star Charts', 'Time Out', training the child to obey and to respect boundaries.

In fact, feeling loved and in control is far more important for childhood discipline than rule-making and punishment. At the heart of the matter is that a sense of being satisfied only comes from having demands met: needy, aggressive behaviour comes from feeling dissatisfied. Likewise, true independence grows out of having felt safely dependent. If a child has been asked to be too independent at too young an age, he actually ends up being needy and dependent later on, which can take the form of aggressive disobedience or clingy whining.

5. Topping up the love when you get home

Once you get back from the two days away, you need to set aside half an hour every evening of more Special Time (or whatever name has been given to the experience). That seems to be all it takes to reignite the safe feeling. Initially your child might just demand to watch the telly with you, but that can be fine if you make it a joint, cuddly experience. Often children will start like that and then be open to playing games or just chatting.

Your child may also benefit from a physical reminder – a memento – of the Special Time, like a shell or a stone from a beach, or maybe a teddy. The object becomes a safe haven in stormy weather. When he flies off the handle or sulks, you can get the memento out and talk about the Special Time, using it as a prop to remind him of that calmer, better time together.

HOW TO GET WHAT YOU NEED
OUT OF THIS BOOK

Since most parents will naturally want to see how the method applies to the problems of their child, I have organized the chapters according to type of problem, as reflected in the chapter titles. Each chapter contains at least one story of a parent who did LB with a child with that problem. The story titles themselves refer to the problems more specifically, as can be seen in the list of stories on pages xi–xii.

The example in the section above illustrates LB done with two nights away, but for all sorts of reasons plenty of parents have done it at different frequencies. Some have done one night, some a single day or several single days, others have created shorter bursts of LB, sometimes as short as just half an hour, repeated over months. By reading the examples in this book, you can decide for yourself what suits you, your child and your practical circumstances:

♥ For stories about doing LB for **two nights away**, turn to Stories 1 (page 27), 2 (page 37), 6 (page 73), 11 (page 126), 17 (page 178) and 18 (page 190).

♥ For stories about **one night away**, go to Stories 3 (page 44), 5 (page 66), 7 (page 86), 8 (page 94) and 20 (page 216).

♥ For stories about **awaydays**, go to Stories 4 (page 54), 9 (page 104) and 19 (page 213).

♥ If you are intrigued by the idea of doing LB in **short bursts**, then stories about this are collected in Chapter Nine (page 155).

♥ Accounts of doing LB **at home** are found in Stories 10 (page 116), 12 (page 156), 13 (page 162), 14 (page 164) 15 (page 167) and 16 (page 168).

♥ Associated with LB at home, accounts about **spending little or no money** on LB are found in Stories 8 (page 94), 9 (page 104), 10 (page 116), 12 (page 156), 13 (page 162), 14 (page 164), 15 (page 167) and 16 (page 168).

You may also wish to look for stories about children who are of a similar age to your own child:

♥ Stories about **children aged 3–6**: Stories 2 (page 37), 3 (page 44), 4 (page 54), 5 (page 66), 9 (page 104), 14 (page 164), 15 (page 167) and 16 (page 168).

♥ Stories about **children aged 7–9**: Stories 6 (page 73), 7 (page 86), 8 (page 94), 11 (page 126), 12 (page 156), 13 (page 162), 14 (page 164) and 20 (page 216).

♥ Stories about **children aged 10–13**: Stories 1 (page 27), 10 (page 116), 17 (page 178), 18 (page 190) and 19 (page 213).

You may personally be in a special situation, such as being a single parent or having relationship problems with your partner, in which case the following stories will be of interest:

♥ If you are a **single parent**, you may also be interested to read stories where others in your position have done LB: Stories 1 (page 27), 8 (page 94), 10 (page 116) and 19 (page 213).

♥ If you feel that **disharmonious relations with a partner** caused your child's problems, you may be interested to see how LB can help: Stories 1 (page 27), 8 (page 94) and 10 (page 116). Story 17 (page 178) illustrates how hard it can be for LB to work if parental rows continue after the LB.

If your child had been born prematurely, then these stories may be of interest to you:

♥ Stories about **children who were born preterm**: Stories 9 (page 104) and 11 (page 126).

The final four stories (Stories 17–20, in Chapter Ten, page 177) are examples of difficulties that arose that meant the LB did not have a lasting effect. These are included to help you understand situations where the improvement after the LB was rapidly reversed on returning to normal life or the LB failed because the parent was unable to carry it out fully. I would recommend all readers to look at these stories because they will help you to avoid potential pitfalls.

FREQUENTLY ASKED QUESTIONS

Do I need to be rich to do LB?

Most definitely not. For examples of LB that required little or no additional expenditure, see Stories 8 (page 94), 9 (page 104) and 10 (page 116) and those in Chapter Nine (page 155).

Where there are two parents, which of them should do the LB?

There is no reason why a father should not do the LB, but in the vast majority of cases it has been the mother. Fathers very frequently get involved in the Top-Ups on return, and in some cases, if the LB includes a night away, fathers do LB with a child who has been left behind. But it seems that in nearly all cases, it is the mother who feels the need for the LB and who also feels that she is the one who wants to change her relationship with a particular child. This can be because she feels his difficulties stem from her current or early relationship with the child, things like early bonding having been interfered with because he had been born preterm and was very small. Since the mother usually is and has been the main carer, she often feels it is best that the LB zone of special affection and control is created with her, so she can use it to help her child when they both return from the zone to ordinary life.

How do I decide which length of time for LB is right for my child?

Practicalities may decide this for you. If you have a baby and there is no one else who could care for him, it is out of the question for you to take an older child away for a night. If you have no partner and more than one child, then nights away may be practically or financially out of the question. Either awaydays or the shorter variants described in Chapter Nine are likely to be most applicable.

In many cases, the more extreme the child's problem, the stronger the case for trying to get two nights away from the family home. There seems to be a greater chance of making the child feel that this is a new beginning, a clean slate, if you go somewhere else. For very troubled children, it may take longer to reverse the patterns, although there are some striking examples of rapid and substantial changes in behaviour following just one night or an awayday (see Story 8, page 94, a single mother).

One of the most dramatic results is reported in Story 11 (page 126), an 8-year-old girl with autistic characteristics. Her mother found that she achieved major changes by carrying out no fewer than five LB weekends away (two nights) over an 18-month period, along with regular and unusually prolonged Top-Ups. In this case, sustained and repeated LB work seemed necessary.

Another thing to bear in mind is the age of the child. On the whole, 3- to 6-year-olds seem to be more malleable, more easily changed. Stories 2 (page 37) and 4 (page 54) are examples of rapid transformations in children under 5 years.

As the child gets older, it may be more and more difficult to alter ingrained habits and patterns, in the parents as well as in the child. However, there are reports of considerable success in children as old as 11 (Story 10, page 116) and 12 (Story 1, page 27) years.

Another consideration is what sort of relationship you have with your child and how much you think you will be able to tolerate. Some parents have reached a point where they dread the child coming home from school because he is so badly behaved. This should not put you off. The mother in Story 1 (page 27) felt like that, but she managed to create a life-changing LB experience with her 12-year-old son. Likewise, the mother in Story 10 (page 116) was extremely worried about her son but did not let that put her off.

Having said all this, it is worth reading the stories in Chapter Nine. They describe a variety of highly imaginative applications of the basic principles of LB which involve no prolonged single periods away from home. In one case (Story 16, page 168), the mother created her own brand of LB play therapy at home with her child.

What sort of problems will be helped by LB?

Even the happiest, most well-adjusted children will have some glitches in their make-up, so all – or almost all – will benefit to some degree from LB. If nothing else, both parent and child will emerge feeling closer and in a good place, emotionally.

Whilst I do not believe that LB can directly change certain problems, such as dyspraxia or severe autism, even these are likely to benefit in that secondary relationship difficulties and lack of self-esteem frequently arise as a fallout from those core problems. LB can help to improve the relationship, confidence and well-being of almost all children.

The main obstacles to LB succeeding, as described in the stories in Chapter Ten, are practicalities or ingrained difficulties of the parents. For example, Story 17 (page 178) involves a mother who regards herself as a 'control freak'. She was unable to overcome that tendency enough to do LB fully. Another common difficulty is where parents are locked into rancorous, disharmonious relationships with each other. Story 18 (page 190) entails such a couple, whose turbulence had created disturbance in their daughter. Although the LB worked, on return to the family home the parental disharmony continued and the girl relapsed back into her distressed state.

How do I deal with jealousy from siblings who feel the target child is getting preferential treatment (favouritism)?

Whilst a lot of parents fear this will be the response, in the event, they are pleasantly surprised that the siblings of the target child tend not to feel disfavoured. This seems to be because the siblings are so delighted that on return from the LB their brother or sister is so much better company, not to mention the parent. In many cases, older siblings are able to grasp that the troubled child needs to be cut some slack. Their reward is a less cranky or angry or difficult sibling.

Having said this, in a few cases the family have settled into a highly destructive pattern that the siblings are unable to let go of. Story 18 (page 190) is one such example. Alas, a combination of continued parental disharmony and rivalrous siblings meant that the child was unable to sustain the benefits that had come from LB.

Several parents have dealt with the problem by promising siblings that they will also have an LB experience. Sometimes it is a partner who provides it. Since LB would be beneficial to nearly all children, this is a splendid solution, if the parents have the time and energy to provide it.

Whilst doing the LB and giving my child control, are there any limits I should set?

Having raised expectations when selling the idea to your child, it is important to spell out that not everything is acceptable. Behaviour that is dangerous to him or to others will not be allowed. If he is rude or antisocial, perhaps to other children, he needs to be finessed, using diplomacy rather than coercion. You can make a bit of a joke of it, and you can use hugs. If he is making fantastical demands, like going to Australia for the day, you can turn that into a fantasy game, in which you play out what would happen: the going on the airplane, meeting kangaroos, being upside down and so on (if you live in Australia and he wants to visit London, the same principle can be applied, only replacing kangaroos with the Queen).

If your child is repeatedly rude and obnoxious in public places, it's best to stay in private ones and ride this out in his relationship to you. You can soak up his behaviour and, by being shown love, he will nearly always come around, eventually.

Will LB work if I am a bit of a control freak?

LB could be especially beneficial to both you and your child. If you can stand it, LB will force you to 'let go' and see that some of your attempts to set rules or interfere with your child are unnecessary. In all probability, you will manage that fine, because you will see your child blossoming during the LB period. Best of all, when you get home, you may well feel able to parent differently.

Story 10 (page 116) is an especially heart-warming example of a mother who managed to do this. Her perfectionist, emotionally withdrawn son flourished following their LB period of 24 hours spent at home.

Of course, your need for control may be so great that you are unable to cope with the experience, as sadly illustrated in Story 17 (page 178). In such cases, it may be advisable, to begin with, to keep the LB periods short. Hopefully, they will highlight to you the difficulties you have and encourage you to seek help for them.

Will LB work if I am too permissive as a parent?

Children do need to have boundaries set for them. Parents who are either boundaryless or inconsistent in their setting of rules create a lot of difficulties for their children.

If you know yourself to be someone who has trouble with boundary-setting, LB may not be appropriate. The problem would be that you have created an environment in which your child is unsure what is acceptable, so giving them total control might only serve to reinforce the idea that 'anything goes'. Parenting classes may well help you to understand why you find it hard to set limits.

However, I would be careful before labelling yourself as too permissive or assuming that problems in your child are the result of having been too lenient. It is extremely common today for experts to mistake lack of boundaries in an older child for what are really the consequences of feeling needy and insecure, as a result of things like a difficult pregnancy or birth or being born underweight because preterm.

If a child who is over 3 is still behaving like a toddler when frustrated – the red mist – many experts believe this is because you have not been rewarding and punishing in a consistent fashion. That can, of course, be true, particularly in chaotic families, whether in low-income sink estates or among the affluent.

But in a home where that is not the case, it is a total misreading of what is really going on. The child is effectively still experiencing things in the way that a toddler does. He is still finding delaying gratification difficult in certain situations. He is feeling neglected, unloved, insecure, 'it's not fair', like a toddler, seeing himself as the centre of the universe, where everything should revolve around him. This will usually be very uneven, so he can be mature and lovable in other situations, but at home his 'pause' button is not working.

Some parents who have been very loving mistake their affectionate approach for permissiveness. Before you slap that label on yourself, consider carefully what happened in your child's early history. That, not lack of 'discipline', may be the true cause of the faulty 'pause' button.

What are the categories of parent
who should not attempt LB?

Abusive parents who are still liable to lose their tempers and lash out should not do LB. Substance-abusing parents are also unlikely to be able to do LB for any sustained periods, although short versions may be possible. It hardly needs saying that if a wife, say, has even the slightest suspicion that her husband might be behaving in a sexually inappropriate way towards their child, then she should never allow him to be involved in LB.

Can carers of adopted or fostered children do LB?

To the best of my knowledge, this has not yet been attempted, although many professionals have suggested to me that the method could have huge potential for carers of adopted or fostered children. In theory, it could be a means of establishing a bond with the child. It could also help in resetting the emotional thermostats of children who are liable to have had disturbing early experiences.

If the child has suffered severe maltreatment for many years, the carer should be realistic about how much will be achieved. Nonetheless, even in these extreme cases, the latest evidence on brain plasticity gives grounds for optimism about improved outcomes.

What is the highest age at which LB
is still appropriate?

Several parents whose children have already entered puberty have asked if LB still might work then.

On the positive side, recent findings suggest that during the pubescent period the brain is especially plastic, undergoing major changes. That could mean that the right parent doing the right things with the right child could have success.

On the negative side, there is considerable potential for a pubescent child to feel confused and intruded upon by the method. Each parent would have to judge this according to his or her relationship, the nature of the problem and the child's personality.

One parent who had done LB with a younger child also tried a version of it on her 18-year-old daughter, with some success. She reported it like this:

> I took her for one night, two days, when she was selecting her university, just before her gap year began. We went for a spa and had a girly night. She was very aware this was the end of her time at home, so that was very nice. She was about to leave for four months.
>
> She selected where we would go and how we spent the day; it was similar to doing it with her younger sister. She wasn't as innocent and 'in her own world' because, being 18, she obviously had a more adult perspective. But it was very enjoyable, and I think she felt it was a very special time. She kept taking photos, her way of recording things, trying to capture those moments.
>
> It had a very special quality, although it's hard to separate that from the fact that we knew she was about to go away. It did seem she was more positive when we got home, but it might have felt like that anyway because she was in the bubble of getting ready to go travelling, the feeling of the last time we would be doing this. The dynamic between her and her sister was more positive afterwards. Would it have been as positive without the weekend? No, I don't think so.

It is likely that LB with older teenagers is never going to have as dramatic an effect as with younger children. However, it clearly can be a valuable way to foster a closer relationship, different from simply having 'quality time'.

Can LB work with twins?

Yes it can, as Story 9 (page 104) shows. However, for the twin in Story 20 (page 216) there was no success, although this does not seem to have had anything to do with the fact that the target child was a twin.

A number of rules for doing LB with twins have emerged:

1. Explain it to both of them at the same time, and that both are going to get it.

2. It is worth bearing in mind that a considerable amount of the difference between twins has been shown by good studies to be caused in the womb (for the scientifically minded, see *Twins: From Fetus to Child* by Alessandra Piontelli). When contemplating LB with twins, it is useful to realize that even though they may be genetically identical, their very different experiences may have made them very different, meaning they require unique LB programmes.

3. It is important to make sure they have understood that both of them are going to get a chance at LB. Perhaps while the mother is doing LB with one twin, the partner (if there is one) could be doing it with the other. It is important they do not feel it's a swizz if one of them gets to go with the mother, because at the deepest level most children will feel that they want recognition from Mum. You need to present it as LB for each from both parents. If necessary, you may need to agree to swap round and give each a chance with both parents.

4. The twins may find it hard to come up with a plan for the LB because, unused to independence, they are so used to

thinking as one person. If possible, talk about it individually with each of them.

5. It can be confusing where both parents do LB with each child. It may be vital that they have different labels for the LB with each parent. Because of the tendency for lack of differentiation with identical twins, you need to beware of them having the same words and phrases. The most important thing is that they choose a special term for their time with you, and one that is different from their sibling's.

6. If you are going away, this is going to be a pretty radical experience for the twin, and probably, for you. It is an opportunity for the twin to start the job of working out who he is, independent of his sibling. This may be their first experience of having an autonomous existence.

7. On the first night, it is likely to be a new experience to be alone in the bed with you. This is a chance for him to feel uniquely cuddled, not part of a group hug. It may seem odd at first, but that is nothing to worry about.

8. Being experienced as uniquely lovable will be a new event. Normally, the affection is being distributed between them, a sense of your divided attention. Previously, there may always have been a measure of confusion about whether you love one twin or the sibling. If cuddling one, it is liable to be the case that the other will be saying, 'When are you going to sit on my bed/read me my story/give me my milk?'

9. On return, the establishment of Top-Up time will inevitably require greater organization than normal. This is easier if you have a cooperative partner, but finding a helper, like a parent or a friend, might just be possible. If the worst comes to the worst, stick the other twin in front of the TV with some popcorn!

10. The memento of the LB could be particularly important in helping to get your child back into the LB zone – it is something unique to remind him of the experience.

ONWARDS AND UPWARDS

That is all you need to know. If you now turn to the chapter describing your child's kind of problem, you can get a feel for how it can work. After reading that chapter, depending on what issues you are still not clear about – like what length of time to create for the LB zone – look through the other stories in the book for examples of how other parents have gone about it. The full list of all the stories and their page numbers can be found at the beginning of the book, on pages xi–xii.

The checklist of things you need to do

♥ Work out what length of time you will do LB
♥ Set a date for when you will do it, at least a week in advance
♥ Sell it to your child, big-time
♥ Get your child to plan what he wants to do during the LB, and get this written down
♥ Get your child to give the experience a name
♥ Do the LB
♥ Do the Top-Ups

Further help

For more information on how other parents have found the experience, there are a host of websites on which LB has been discussed, including some in Australia and the United States, as well as in Britain. If you put the keywords 'love bombing psychologist oliver james' into Google, it will bring up thousands of results for you to explore (but ignore the entries relating to a cult that uses 'love bombing' to seduce new members!).

In addition, you can go to the official Love Bombing website (**www.lovebombing.info**). Apart from sharing stories of what to do and problem-solving with other parents, you can also contact Oliver James through that site (you can also contact him through **www.oliver-james-books.com**).

TWO

Temper tantrums, defiance, raging

It takes time for children to learn how to tolerate frustration of their wishes without becoming furious. It is completely natural for small children to use physical force to impose their will and for them to become incensed when thwarted.

Left to play in the company of other toddlers, the average 18-month-old will try to take a toy off another eight times an hour. He will still do so three times an hour when he is a year older than that.

It is only gradually that the child learns that not only is this reaction unacceptable, it is distressing for his peers. The capacity for self-regulation – the ability to press a 'pause' button before taking physical action – has to evolve slowly. The part of the brain responsible (called the Orbitofrontal Cortex) develops as a result of being responded to by carers, starting at birth. Over the succeeding couple of years, the responsiveness of the carer manages the child's emotions. If the child is hungry or sad or angry, sympathetic tuning-in by the carer enables the child to recover. Many thousands of tiny experiences of such responsiveness gradually enable the child to become more aware of his own feelings through his thoughts, giving him the potential for self-control. But until he has language and a relatively sophisticated mind, he is still prone to being swamped by emotion – the 'red mist' coming down and the temper tantrums of the terrible twos (see Sue Gerhardt's book *The Selfish Society* for a more detailed account of this; see also her book *Why Love Matters*).

If the consequences of his actions are constantly explained to the child ('if you hit that child, he won't like it') and if he is consistently shown love and support and sympathy for his predicament, he will come to be able to know his own feelings and feel safe enough that his needs will be met without having to impose himself.

If there are problems early on, such as if the baby is very difficult from birth on and seems unmanageable to a hard-pressed mother, or if the parents are constantly rowing and unable to tune into the baby as much as they would like, or if a younger sibling takes up all the mother's attention, or if the mother is depressed, then the development of the pause button, the braking system of emotions, is impeded. The child may be good as gold sometimes, perhaps forced to be so at school or in other contexts, but it may also be a 4- or 6- or 10- or 12-year-old who has toddler meltdowns at home. If he does not have his needs met immediately, like a toddler he is incensed and swamped by emotion.

Once this cycle of fury has got underway, the child can seem permanently 'naughty', constantly behaving badly when with the parent. He may be surly, snarling, whingeing, brittle-tempered, and the parent feels sucked into a pattern of over-control, spending all day nagging and 'nattering' – drawn into micromanagement, finding themselves saying 'put that down', 'let go of your brother', 'behave yourself!' so often that the punitive currency is devalued.

Using conventional methods for controlling the child

simply do not work for most such children, or else they produce a false, temporary performance of goodness with a subversive fury that is never far from the surface. Naughty steps, fridge charts, time out in the bedroom, these may briefly and superficially alter the behaviour, but they mainly help in protecting the parent from losing her temper. That is valuable, because in these situations, as a parent, it's jolly hard not to turn into a toddler yourself, easily losing your temper and becoming red-faced with rage. But there is an alternative to these taming-the-beast-in-the-nursery methods, one that does ultimately help the child to learn where the boundaries are.

For some parents, LB seems to be a way to set off in a new direction. It not only gives the child a sense of being loved and in control, feelings he may have lacked when much smaller, it also helps the parent to remember why she was glad to have given birth to someone who has become a little terror. When the parent now sets boundaries, the child actually listens! The new pattern is such a relief for both parties, as the stories in this chapter illustrate.

STORY 1

Two nights away – single mother
A son who replicates his father's anger attacks: Sean, aged 12

Sean, 12, has a brother, Terry, who is four years younger. His mother, Carrie, separated from her husband, Brian, when Sean was 5. Brian was prone to tempestuous rages, although never physically violent to Carrie.

Sean's problems

Sean gets very, very angry. This happens frequently and is making Carrie scared. Recently, he smashed a glass door. He cruelly bullies his little brother, Terry, which particularly upsets Carrie because she was a bullied little sister herself. She finds it unbearable that she cannot always protect Terry. She dreads Sean coming home from school because he is now tall, strong and threatening. On one occasion, she had to lock herself and Terry in her van to escape from Sean, so fearful was she.

These tyrannical attacks are not a daily event; the rest of the time the family can get along fine. Sean is applying himself at school and has plenty of friends. The explosions only seem to happen in relation to the family.

Carrie says that 'He is quite a dominant boy. I have caught him in the street walking to school with the TV remote control in his hand – his solution to the battle for who decides what to watch. He will call himself the man of the house, and I will say, "Okay, in that case you can help me put out the rubbish and look after your little brother, that's part of the job of being man of the house." He didn't much like that idea!'

Planning the LB

Carrie put it to Sean like this: 'We're never on our own any more – how about you and me go somewhere and do something? You get to choose what we do.' Somewhat to her surprise, considering how hostile he often is, he loved the idea.

They talked about lots of different possible schemes. Although on a modest income, Carrie had recently inherited some money from a grandparent, so she asked if he would like a package weekend in a foreign capital, like Rome. She tried really hard not to make it somewhere she wanted, and luckily Rome appealed to Sean.

During the next three weeks, they researched the things they could do and where they might stay. Carrie tried not to do this in front of Terry, to avoid provoking jealousy. Terry was going to spend the weekend with his father, who had just had a new baby with a new partner. Carrie worried that leaving him in that situation might make him feel excluded.

Sean was full of excited anticipation of all the firsts: going to stay in a hotel, going on a plane, having his mother to himself. Because it was Italy, it was going to be ice creams, pizza and pasta, so he was looking forward to his favourite foods. They watched *Angels & Demons*, about killer priests and Roman Catholic conspiracies, and they looked up the Vatican and the Coliseum on the Internet.

The weekend

Just going to an airport was a thrill for Sean. Looking around it, buying stuff for the plane, and the first experience of travelling on one were all 'awesome'. Installed in the modest hotel, Sean could not wait to explore the city.

Carrie quickly felt that the experience was a total contrast from their normal lives, and the difference was not so much to do with being in a foreign land. She recalls that 'Giving the control to him made me realize how orchestrated their lives are. On the first night we saw a lovely restaurant where the locals went, but he wanted the touristy place next door. I had to give in and say, "Fine, we'll go there." He loved deciding stuff. There were a couple of moments, like a taxi driver ripping us off, where I could be the adult and say, "Don't worry, I'll deal with it." Then it was back to "now you get to choose" again.'

With Sean left to make all the choices, on one day they went twice to the Vatican, morning and evening. She recalls that 'We had really good fun zooming around there. He's very anti-religious and anti-war whereas I am interested in comparative religion. The Pope was speaking in front of a life-size nativity, which Sean scoffed at. Nonetheless, he was fascinated by the mixture of beauty and incongruous details.' There were policemen with guns, and you had to go through x-ray machines to get in. They went up to the top of the Cupola and looked out over Rome. He made a video on his phone, giving a humorous running commentary as they made their way back down the winding steps. When they went into St Peter's, he took pictures of the Virgin Mary and put a scarf round her neck. The guards in their Armani suits seemed unconcerned. She enjoyed his strident critique of what he was seeing: 'As we left, he was asking "What on earth's this got do with Jesus, all this pomp and circumstance?" – quite rightly, in my view. Outside, there were beggars next-door to franchises selling little baby Jesuses.'

In the evening, they wandered out looking for somewhere to eat and ended up walking through the ancient part of the centre of town. They ate some pizza and pasta. Strolling for miles, they ended up back at the Vatican. Says Carrie, 'I just let him lead me around. He made great choices. For instance, everyone said, "Don't go to the Vatican on Sunday, it will be very crowded", but he was right, it was the perfect time to go – even the weather was good!'

The 'frequent expression of love' component of the LB also went well, even though Sean was 12 years old. Carrie commented that 'We're quite a huggy family anyway. My boys are very affectionate, but I gave him lots of hugs. It's really funny now – we say "I love you"', he says "Love you" back. It's like a little reminder, he's right there with that, even if we're both being really grumpy.'

There was one point when Sean wanted to see the Catacombs, not knowing that they are shut for two hours during lunch. There was no one around, so they found a bus shelter with a hot chocolate machine and cuddled for about an hour and a half. Carrie says it was 'To keep warm and because it's nice to have a cuddle. It did feel like remembering being in love again with a baby. I was reminded, too, how interesting he is and how much I love him, how always having to be in control and be The Adult gets in the way.'

She also realized the extent to which Sean had felt displaced by the arrival of his younger brother. She says that 'At the end he said, "Look, see, when Terry isn't here, everything's fine." He decided that the problem was his little brother. I did feel when I had my second child it was like being unfaithful.'

They shared a room with twin beds. On the Sunday morning she got up earlier than he; he wanted a lie-in, so she brought him a roll. They watched a bit of Italian telly, which they thought was hilarious.

Somehow the experience never got a special name; it is referred to just as 'When we went to Rome'. He sings a silly song called 'Basilica' in a high voice that he made up to annoy her. However, she has many photos of the weekend that she has put up in the kitchen and in his room. Carrie feels that photographs of good experiences are helpful. She recalls that 'My sister doesn't remember a single good thing about our childhood, but I do, because I have some photos of good experiences. I like to have happy photos up.' Sean has photos of them at the Trevi Fountain on his Facebook page. They did not bring back any mementos, although he had bought some rudely shaped pasta, which he thought very funny.

The Top-Ups

Much to Carrie's delight, Sean actively asked for the Top-Ups, calling them Our Time. He is an X-Box addict, and sometimes he will play during the Top-Up and then, at the end, go 'Oh, this was Our Time', as if he regrets not having taken the opportunity to be with Carrie. They have kept the Our Time going. She will turn off her computer and her phone, and they will hang out together doing whatever he wants. She says, 'We have always had "Blanky Time" as a family, watching movies on the sofa in a big heap together, under a blanket. But this is different because it's just him and me.'

The effects of the LB

Carrie was amazed at the rapidity and extent of the change in Sean. 'I was very surprised that the anger attacks stopped so quickly. It's giving him the feeling of control, producing self-control and then a really proper apology, calm.'

Recently, he went so far as to describe the change in himself as 'an awakening'. She says, 'If he does get angry, he calms down much more quickly and then says "sorry" and really means it. I say "I love you" and he says "I love you too, Mum". Then we have a hug and a kiss.'

She is also astonished at how much more insightful he has become. 'He's been really noticing how he behaves towards me and that it isn't alright. He said, "When I talk to you, I swear a lot. It's become a habit." I asked, "Do you like doing that?" And he said, "No, I want to stop, but I don't know if I can." That's what he means about an awakening. There has been extreme verbal abuse – the worst things you can ever imagine anyone saying to you – and this from a 12-year-old, very shocking. But now the word "respect" does come up: he's been much more respectful.'

There has been a drastic improvement in his cooperativeness. 'He's been helping me a lot more around the house. If the dog is at the back door, he will go and let it in and shut the door. He helps to bring the shopping in from the car. He will take the rubbish to the recycling bin at the end of the street. Before, he really would not do anything at all, and it would be dangerous to even ask.'

She accepts that he does sometimes still get angry and that the improvement is a work in progress. 'It's not like we have turned into this different family, we are not "fixed", but it's much, much better. Also, he is nearly 13, and he has been behaving like this for a great many years, which his little brother does copy. He still does go to the extreme places sometimes, but not nearly as much. I used to dread him coming home after he'd been with their Dad.'

She suspects that an important effect of the weekend was on her behaviour. 'The way I relate to him has changed. I asked my sister about this today, and she says the way I treat him has altered, which affects what they are like. I'm much calmer. Like all kids, they have pushed me, but theirs is really extreme behaviour. I did yell on Saturday night and it became briefly how it was before, highlighting how different it is now. I know yelling doesn't work, it creates a war zone.'

She feels they might need to repeat some form of the LB weekend again. 'On three nights last week he came and got in bed with me. He had been behaving badly, tormenting his little brother to wind me up, punching him in the spine. He's a big lad now. It made me realize I need a booster, I need to get back in the LB zone. It's at least as much about me getting into the right place as him. I want to go and look at those pictures and remember what a nice time we had. Maybe we need a little reminder, but it's generally a lot better.'

The causes of Sean's problems

Carrie's mother had been very neglectful of her in the early years, and Carrie was determined to give her sons a different experience to that. She tuned into Sean as a baby and overcame several adversities to provide solid and loving early care. His problems seem to be almost wholly due to his parents' alarmingly acrimonious marriage and separation, when he was aged 5.

Sean's father, Brian, was prone to frequent and extreme anger attacks when with the family. His work took him away for weeks on end, but on return he would be tyrannical. He never hit Carrie, but he would engage in what is called 'intimate terrorism' – a sustained hate campaign. Whilst small, Sean witnessed his father spit at her, swear furiously and throw furniture and other household objects around, a complete loss of control. At such times Brian was terrifying. Carrie was the kind of person who fought back. She would stick up for herself, and the rows would last for hours.

What was more, from around the age of 3 years, Sean was bullied and badgered by Brian. He would shout at him for the smallest thing. Carrie believes Sean was terrified by that, as well as by witnessing his father raging against his mother.

As Sean began to behave with similar cruelty, she had begun to believe there was some kind of genetic bad blood that had been passed from father to son. However, I explained to her that the scientific evidence proves conclusively that violence is not inherited in this way. No difference has ever been demonstrated in the genes of the violent compared with the non-violent, nor do studies of identical twins or adoptees give any reason to suppose that criminal violence is inherited. What the evidence shows emphatically is that it is learnt, partly from observing the father use verbal or physical violence as a way of expressing frustration, modelling it as the right way to deal with anger. At a deeper level, the child is terrified and comes to expect attacks, and is made paranoid. If you expect others to attack you, you go on the offensive.

The definitive study compared boys whose violent fathers left the family with those whose violent fathers remained. Measured 30 years later, the number of convictions for criminal violence was significantly lower if the father had left: sons exposed to violent fathers throughout childhood are much more likely to become violent themselves.

Carrie intuited this. Having persuaded Brian to undergo anger management training, it failed. The point at which she realized she had to make him leave was when he continued to be emotionally abusive to Sean.

She says that Sean's anger attacks are almost indistinguishable in their tone and content from his father's. She found herself dreading Sean's return from school, just as she had dreaded Brian coming home from work. But since the LB weekend, she has realized that the problem is not in the least genetically programmed. Indeed, Sean is well on the way to being cured.

Sean's case is a nice illustration of the extent to which problems are more easily reversible, the later they were caused. He felt loved and secure as a baby and toddler, giving him solid psychological foundations. Through LB, he was able to have an experience of feeling safe and in control. At a deep level, he came to realize that he did not have to see his mother as hostile but as benign – his 'awakening'. Whilst he is still wrestling with understanding that he does not have to behave towards her the way his father did, he is well on the way to realizing that.

Postscript: one year later

Carrie sent me an email updating progress over a year after the LB. It was as follows.

> The original issue that prompted me to contact you, his inappropriate response to stressful situations, specifically people rowing, is definitely a lot better. Of course, he is a big brother, so obviously he likes to wind his brother up.

One thing I really noticed is that he apologizes. Real, proper, heartfelt apologies.

He feels that his outbursts over the last few months have been testosterone-driven, and that has subsided, for now. He is still capable of horrible behaviour and verbal abuse.

But Terry and I used to go and sit in my van and lock ourselves in when Sean got really angry. We haven't done that for a long time.

We talk about our Rome adventure with great fondness. It's something that we'll always have. His little brother is planning a trip with me now: only fair!

One thing I can't change is his Dad, though he's happier at the moment, so things are possibly easier. I'm told at this stage it's normal for Dads and sons to be like stags locking horns. His Dad can't physically dominate him in the same way. Sean is like me in that we stand up for ourselves, but if you live with someone angry and stressful, you have to learn to go quiet and remove yourself, not take it on, or it all just escalates.

I think that Sean and I are at a classic Mum-and-son stage, where you can end up hating each other! Seems like that's what happens at 13. Luckily we just have bouts of that. It interests me that the 12/13-year mark is when marriages break up, and it seems to me that the relationship between mothers and sons seems to mirror that.

I've got rid of *Modern Warfare 3* on the X-Box. Horrible game, I should never have had it in the house – I didn't want to, but I gave in to parent peer pressure! I think it affected his behaviour. We still have fights about its absence, but they're not so bad now.

Maybe I can sum up: there is a definite change, and there is still a lot to work on. I can't do anything about a lot of the influences in his life, or the past. Or change his Dad.

I try and stay calm, but I'm a champion shouter when pushed, and far from perfect. And we know we love each other. And he loves his Dad.

STORY 2

Two nights away
Hostile rejection of mother: Tanya, aged 4

Tanya, 4, has a brother two years younger than she. Their mother, Jill, has cared for them full-time from birth and is happily married.

This was one of the most straightforwardly successful LB cases reported to me. Jill sent me an email stating, 'I just wanted to say thank you for your idea of Love Bombing. Tanya sobbed in the car all the way home because she didn't want to leave and when we got home she asked for more "Mummy Time". This was a huge shock for me, as I felt like I was the last person she wanted to be around by her previous behaviour.' Subsequently interviewed on the phone, Jill said, 'I was really surprised, it was quite amazing. She's gone from being a 4-year-old going on 16, angsty and troublesome, to being lovely.'

Tanya's problems

Jill said that 'There's always a destructiveness to her, trying to wind me up, even though I am the most calm, patient person.' Indeed, Jill's voice on the phone had a quiet, low-key delivery, no drama to its tone or volume, no extravagance in her choice of words.

Tanya was constantly defiant, persistently stand-offish and rejecting of Jill. She said, 'Nothing was ever quite enough. We would get through so many activities, and it was never enough. She never was calm, could not settle, always wanted more, but I never knew what she wanted: does she need more activities? More time with her friends? I couldn't work out what it was.'

Planning the LB

Jill announced that they were going to a hotel in a nearby town for a couple of nights. She gave Tanya completely free choice within the limitation of not having a car and keeping within walking distance of the hotel, near the town centre.

Tanya was clear what she would like to do: a visit to the cinema, the toyshop, a particular café, a trip on a bus, the park. She was resolved in her mind about all this, had it planned out, scheduled a time for everything. When Jill mentioned a prehistoric castle, she showed no interest.

Jill forgot to suggest that she choose a name for the experience, but from towards the end Tanya started calling it Mummy Time, which is what she calls it now. She has added Daddy Time to that, because sometimes he does the Top-Ups.

The LB weekend

The Friday

Jill was not in the mood for doing LB because that morning she had found out that a friend's wife had died suddenly. But having booked the hotel, they went.

Jill took her to the supermarket to choose her favourite foods.

They stockpiled crisps, sweets, chocolate milk drinks, but Tanya was surprisingly restrained. Jill was saying 'Do you want more than that, is that it? Really?' Tanya picked whatever she wanted without being greedy.

They spent the first afternoon watching television, having snacks. Then they went out to the park and found some stepping-stones. Tanya did some running around, but she was quite quiet. Jill kept looking at her and thinking, 'I'm not sure she's enjoying this.' She was expecting her to be more cheerful.

When they got back to the hotel, Tanya asked to have a bath and for her hair to be washed. Then Jill read her a story and tucked her up in bed, but she took ages to fall asleep because she was so excited.

Tanya suffers from reflux (lying flat causes her to feel nauseous and to burp). Her sleep was quite disturbed because the bed was arranged too flat. Tanya kept waking, with Jill trying to sort the pillows to prop her up so that she was sleeping in a raised posture. Nonetheless, Tanya was happy enough, excited, and she was not bothered by the noise of a wedding reception going on in the hotel.

The Saturday

They had breakfast in the room, watching TV. Then Tanya sorted her jewellery; she had brought all of it with her, along with all of Jill's. This kept her riveted, trying it on.

On schedule, they went to the cinema, to the toyshop, had a look around the town, went for a coffee, a walk and then, when Tanya was tired, got a taxi back to the room. There they played her favourite games. For supper they went out to a restaurant and had chips. Jill was surprised that 'She really enjoyed it, actually, because normally she plays up in restaurants, quite hard work.

Because there were only two of us, it was quite different. She was chatty and calm, still quite quiet. She was quiet all day, I was expecting her to be more openly cheerful and kept wondering if she was enjoying it or not.'

In their normal life, Jill regularly tells Tanya that she loves her, and she did not do too much of that during the LB because 'Every time I said it she just looked at me, as if she was questioning why I was doing it so much. But I have found that since we got back, she has been a lot more receptive to it. She doesn't snub me. She's letting me do that now.'

On the second night, it took ages for Tanya to go to sleep because she was so excited. She kept jumping out of bed and running around. Jill thinks that 'She was partly testing to see how much she could get away with. She would say she needed a drink or to go to the bathroom, then it was "the light's too bright", "the light's too dark". She got me to go into the bathroom and then to come out, then asked me to do it again. Eventually, after a couple of hours, I had to say, "I am going to stay here until you fall asleep", and she dropped off quite quickly. I mentioned that she might be too tired to do the activities she had planned on the schedule. We normally stay with her anyway to get her to sleep, usually my husband.'

The Sunday

They had breakfast and went to the toyshop because Tanya wanted to buy some bubbles. They went to the park that Tanya had found, happy doing bubbles for much of the morning. When they had to get back to the hotel to check out, Tanya said she didn't want to leave, and that was when she used the words Mummy Time, not wanting it to end. Recalls Jill, 'She just seemed so happy. It was like she had really let go.'

The Top-Ups

They have always had time on their own together when Tanya's brother has his morning and afternoon naps. These times have been transformed, says Jill: 'A lot, lot, lot better. The time we get is lovely, she plays with me. I think she sees the things I do differently, as well. If I'm not too responsive, she says "come on Mummy, come on Mummy" instead of getting cross with me, which is encouraging. Now she feels I do want to be with, and to play with, her. Previously she would have got stand-offish, with-drawn, or angry and stroppy. Once she was like that, I felt even less like playing and ended up putting a wash on or cooking. I would often be annoyed from the morning anyway in the past, having to cajole her into her clothes and to eat breakfast.'

The impact of the LB on Tanya

Reporting back three months later, Jill said that 'It was bizarre. Just that weekend really did seem to press a "reset" button. She has a different personality as a result of it. A lot of things about her didn't make any sense at all, and it was suddenly, "Ah, yes, I see why."'

She has become affectionate towards Jill and is able to relax for the first time, being happy and cuddly. In the past, if asked to do something, she would immediately be defiant. Jill says that 'Now it's totally different, it feels like we started again, a fresh start. Now that she is calmer, it's easier to get through to her, request her to do things. So I am a lot calmer too – a knock-on effect for everyone. She gets dressed in the morning, is cooperative, and knows that we will be able to play later on, she understands that now. I remind her that we will be having Mummy Time later on.'

A year and a half after the LB, I received the following update:

Positive changes have continued. She has continued to become more sociable, outgoing and a completely different personality at home. In the month after I spoke to you she got invited to two parties by children she had made friends with herself (instead of children of my friends). She is nearly at the end of her reception year at school and she absolutely loves it, she has made lots of friends in her class and the years above, she is one of the top in her class in literacy, she is a very confident, happy and strong character. Her teacher said that she is very sociable, enjoys 'show and tell', volunteers for using the interactive board in front of the class and helps less confident children in their schoolwork. That's completely different from 18 months ago when she refused to talk or look at the staff at her preschool and wouldn't join in the group activities.

One of the most significant things during the weekend was that she invented a baby alter ego. Following this, whenever she has a transition during her day she pretends to be the baby and makes baby noises. Her favourite position is being cradled with lots of eye contact (the usual mother–baby position). When she was a baby she spent nearly all her waking time on a shoulder screaming/crying and missed out on the most basic interaction between parents and child.

The alter ego appears less now. The more sociable she becomes, the easier daily transitions seem to her.

Both my children still have silent reflux, it still wakes them up at night and both still have feeding issues because of it, but it is vastly better than it was. The improvement in her reflux will have made a huge difference to her – her sleep deprivation was significant then, and she was anxious about eating food (now she is just very, very fussy about it!). So how much of the change is the lovebombing and how much is the reflux, I don't know, but the lovebombing made an enormous change and she still keeps asking if the four of us as a family can go back to the hotel we stayed in.

After the lovebombing, my husband and I both had counselling as we both felt traumatized and emotionally shut down from the whole reflux experience. The change in our daughter allowed us the 'head space' to do counselling, and that made a huge difference to our relationship with both children.

One of my friends also tried lovebombing with her son. She took him away to festivals and their relationship completely changed afterwards. She went from being irritated with him all the time and applying for jobs to get away from him, to really enjoying his company and throwing herself into his imaginary role play games.

The causes of Tanya's hostility towards Jill

Both the children suffered from reflux from birth, creating a lot of pain. It has meant that Tanya has always been sleep-deprived, affecting her mood. Then her brother was born with reflux as well. Jill feels that this meant Tanya did not get much attention during his first year: 'I assume that because of her brother's reflux and the attention it has demanded, she feels he has come first.'

This was exacerbated when Tanya went to preschool and was badly bullied by another child. It was after that when Tanya started pushing Jill away and became destructive.

Jill says that 'Feeling in control and putting her plans into action, and that I was prepared to spend that time with her, seemed to wipe that out, made her feel she was very, very special to me.'

Jill has noticed that Tanya has carried on with trying to feel in charge of scheduling. 'We had a friend over recently and she scheduled all the different games they were going to play. She kept asking me what the time was and working out how much she was in sync with her normal routine. She kept on saying things like, "I think we'll have the snack now."'

Overall, it would seem that Jill had a fundamentally good relationship with Tanya in the earliest years, despite the reflux trouble. This was disrupted by the arrival of her brother and his reflux and then by the school bullying. It would seem the LB reset Tanya's relationship to Jill to a loving, safe one, where she became able to assume that her mother loved her and would be a source of enjoyment rather than nagging or neglect.

STORY 3

One night away
Short-fused son, fussy mother likes clear rules: Todd, aged 6

Todd, aged 6, has a sister two years younger than he. Both his parents are doctors; his mother, Sian, is a warm and thoughtful woman, albeit someone who finds the chaos of the early years unsettling, preferring orderliness.

Todd's problems

Todd has extreme reactions to apparently minor instructions or requests to cooperate. He is not badly behaved, on the whole. Sian says, 'He is delightful. But he finds it very hard to regulate, to dampen down his emotions and behaviour when things don't go his way. That is where the eruptions occur, in which he can seem like a toddler having a tantrum, purple-faced with rage, the red mist.'

For example, his sister had been given some sweets, which she agreed to share with him. When she chose the one that she wanted, he flew into a rage because he thought that he should have been able to choose first. He shouted 'Noooooo' and got very, very cross. He is articulate and emotionally literate about it: 'That's not fair! You always say you will be fair when you're not: look how cross you've made me now.' There is lots of blame for how he is feeling which he puts onto other people. And that is despite the fact that if he had sweets and shared them, he would expect to get first choice.

Sian finds herself thinking, 'What on earth have we done wrong here? We've done nothing but bestow love on him, and this is what we get.' She says, 'I have noticed this in children from educated families: not only do they come up with these barrack-room lawyer arguments, pointing out your contradictions, complete with psychological analysis of your motives, they are also physically quite strong and can be jolly hard to manage, to the point of being frightening if you try to physically restrain them. Fast-forward 10 or 15 years and you have a man who can't make sense of what he's feeling and can't control himself. I want to avoid that happening.'

Planning the LB

Todd called it his Special Weekend. He loves planning and was delighted to decide what to do and where to stay. He wrote down a list of all the things he would like to do. This ranged from wanting to buy strawberries to wanting to go to the Thomas Land theme park. He wanted ice cream, crisps, magazines and to go to the Railway Museum, which he had enjoyed before. She was surprised how limited his wish list was, given a totally free choice. Sian suggested places to stay that were near the locations he had identified, and they whittled it down to a shortlist.

The Saturday

They started by going to the supermarket to buy strawberries and raspberries, chocolate muffins, cartons of juice. For Todd it was a very different experience to be able to choose whatever he wanted and as much as he wanted – none of the usual 'you can have one biscuit and then nothing till lunchtime'. Said Sian, 'It was fascinating to see how he responded to being let loose in the proverbial sweet shop. His personality likes being rule-driven, so once he had settled on three muffins, that was enough. He was not interested in excess, just in being in charge.'

They went from there to the Railway Museum, which he enjoyed, then he had his lunch box. He asked, 'Can I dip my crisps in the ketchup?', enjoying being able to try things out, a delight in being able to change the rules. It made Sian question the things she forbids him to do, whether these prohibitions are always necessary.

They drove to the hotel, Todd never having stayed in one before. He wanted to see the room and check in. Although a modest room, he thought it the peak of luxury, the TV, the mini-biscuits. He was very happy to spend time reading his magazines and watching telly. He does not watch much at home, so it was a big thrill to watch as much as he liked and what he chose. He did a bit more planning, then they went out for a pizza.

All day, Sian says, she was trying to envelop him in affection. 'But in the restaurant there were some things I realized that weren't alright, which was quite tricky. So there were things I couldn't let him do in a public place. I didn't want to rain on his parade, spoil the mood, but I had to say, "you do need to sit down" and "it's not okay to behave like that". He was wanting to wander around, but there had to be a point where it was not okay to disrupt other families. And there were some table manners that could not be allowed to pass in public.'

In some respects she was the one with the difficulty, struggling to cope with an ambiguous situation. 'I realized there were lines he could not cross: the rule was "yes, you can do what you want – for most of the time". Of course, his attitude was "but you said I could do whatever I want". I explained that this did not include being rude or inconsiderate to strangers.'

They went back to the hotel and snuggled down to sleep. That was a novelty for him because he has never shared his parents' bed. 'He was never one to clamber into our bed during the night. So that was all very exciting, quite special. When he was little we were conscious of discouraging that habit, and he's always been happy to stay in his own bed. If he had a nightmare he would want comfort, but that was it. So to share the bed was a treat, really. It was nice to snuggle up. I wasn't scared I was going to start him on a new habit, he was old enough to realize this was a treat, and as far as it went, restricted to this context. For that night he enjoyed having my complete attention and cuddling up, cosy.'

They had a reasonably good night's sleep, though Todd woke a few times to check it was all real, that they were still there in a hotel. Breakfast offered the vast selection of different choices, taking as much as he wanted, revelling in that. This was followed by the thrill of heading off to Thomas Land, being able to go on whatever rides he wanted for as long as he wanted. Sian recalls, 'He was so into the whole idea. It was a treat not to have to worry about his sister, and to go on things again and again and again, the rollercoaster repeatedly. After a while he was wanting to do that on his own, in his element.'

He came back from the rollercoaster with a key-ring picture of himself and also with a photo of the two of them in front of it. This has turned into a powerful memento: 'He's got that picture in a little frame now on his wall, and the key ring attached to his school bag. He likes to look at the picture, it reminds him of the weekend.'

Before setting off for home, there was a moment when Todd ran off on his own, and Sian had to be firm with him. His response was, 'Oh you're spoiling my weekend', upset by her changing into someone giving instructions. Sian says that 'He recovered from that much faster than he would have at home; he erupted less because the day held it together for him – he had been in control and felt loved.'

The Top-Ups

They tried to give him an extra half-hour in the evenings by keeping him down after his sister had gone to bed. The aim was to get her off at 7 o'clock and give him the extra half-hour after that. Being seen as different from his sister was a bonus for him. Sian says that 'We were better at it to begin with, but then her bedtime ate into his. We try to split it between my husband and me. I am not sure if he sees that as Mummy Time. Sometimes he will say, "What shall we do in our Extra Time" – he calls it that rather than Special Time. Sometimes he just reads on his own, but sometimes it's together on the sofa.'

She believes that, at first, it reminded him of the weekend. Also, six months after the LB, they had another day away together, which kept it alive. She says the weekend 'is certainly still something he remembers. His sister had a weekend away with her father, and she feels the same about her LB period.'

The effect of the LB on his behaviour

One year later, Sian reports that 'On the day after we got back, there was something that frustrated him and he just completely exploded, went right off the deep end, very cross and upset. But

I think that was because he was having to adjust to returning to the old rules, a reaction to normal day-to-day, "you can't always do what you want" life. But after that, the interesting thing is he has not done it again once, at all, ever, since. It's a year later, and he has not had one of those massive, massive, screaming and shouting and kicking and slamming doors, red-faced toddler-tantrum furies, total meltdowns, which used to be quite frequent before the LB.'

Sian believes that the LB weekend, combined with changes in the way she behaves, is the reason for this. 'His anger never reaches that extreme. He has come down a notch or two, in terms of how far off the deep end he goes. He is still very easily tipped from being fine to becoming cross, or unhappy and moaning. That happens when we say "Come on now, it's time for you to do this or that", but it's not the same height-ened response which was bothering me. His rate of recovery has also speeded up.'

As well as resetting Todd's thermostat, she also believes the improvement results from her and her husband behaving differently. 'We realize we sometimes have made unnecessary demands. For instance, when he is getting dressed in the morn-ing, he will often get caught up in reading a book. That would be a flashpoint: "Come on, do your teeth", or "Get your clothes on". But I realized if I was in the middle of reading a book, I would not want someone barking at me to put it down and do my teeth.'

She feels they had been slightly too rigid about setting limits. 'We like to keep clear lines they cannot cross, but at the same time we want to be flexible, want to show him that flexibility is also a virtue through our example. You're balancing your needs and their needs, and you don't want to be losing control yourself. I am a parent who has tried to keep the boundaries clear, but as he gets older I have to let him have more autonomy.'

She also believes that the end of his explosions is due to her handling them better in the early stages. 'We react differently. I try harder to modulate my reaction. I am constantly trying to de-escalate my emotions, step away and calm myself, to give him an example, help him see that if you take a deep breath and get some distance in time from the event, and mental distance, you can cope with the feelings better. I am wrestling with at what age he can grasp the idea that "I still love you but I don't like that behaviour". To what extent can he comprehend that, rather than thinking "I am that behaviour"? The problem arises when I am changing what he is doing, or if he wants something, like to get a game out, and I am telling him now is not the time. That used to get a huge eruption, if I said "No you can't do that now". It would send him into "Ooooohhhhh". I am staying calmer, on a good day, not allowing an inflation of emotion. I am changing the negative pattern we had got into, made a good dent in it. The morning and night-time routines are the main flashpoints, and I am on that case.'

Sian feels that they are more affectionate, especially Todd. 'The love stuff was unusual, but you could see a point in the day when he was 'yeah, yeah, I know, no need to go on saying it'. But it brought out into the open those things that you don't normally make explicit. I have carried on doing that with both of them. If anything, it's gone a bit the other way, like at night-time he wants to have a cuddle. Now he can't quite get enough of that, because we have always had a bed-time routine. It feels a bit funny, I am not quite sure where to put the boundary on that, maybe because I am someone who likes to put boundaries down. It would be lovely to have time to spend half an hour lying down every night cuddling as he falls asleep. But there are chores to be done, and we can't do that every night. Still, it's important to treasure those precious moments – it won't be long before you are waving them off to university.'

Looking back on the changes, Sian concludes that 'It was a really lovely experience for both of us. It has reduced the intensity of the rage he was showing when frustrated. It's connected us up. We cuddle more.'

The causes of Todd's problems

It is possible that Sian's slightly excessive need to set limits and have rules was winding Todd up. The LB weekend forced her to notice that some of her attempts to control him were a fussy reflection of her discomfort with the unpredictability and uncertainty that inevitably arises where small children are concerned.

Her well-intentioned attempts to create limits had been there from the start. She recalls that 'When he was a little baby we did do controlled crying. As an emotionally vulnerable little boy, that may have left him insecure, too much demand on him to be self-controlled too young.' That may be true. But a more important cause of the massive rages could have been a steady drip-drip of demands on Todd, her attempts to set limits, which ended up as a nagging nattering that enraged him.

WHERE TO GO NEXT IN THE BOOK

Other LB stories that relate to this chapter:

- ♥ **Two nights away:** Stories 6 (page 73), 11 (page 126), 17 (page 178) and 18 (page 190)

- ♥ **One night away:** Stories 5 (page 66), 7 (page 86), 8 (page 94) and 20 (page 216)

Love Bombing

♥ **Awaydays:** Stories 4 (page 54), 9 (page 104) and 19 (page 213)

♥ **At home:** Stories 10 (page 116), 12 (page 156), 13 (page 162), 14 (page 164), 15 (page 167) and 16 (page 168)

♥ **Spending little or no money:** Stories 8 (page 94), 9 (page 104), 10 (page 116), 12 (page 156), 13 (page 162), 14 (page 164), 15 (page 167) and 16 (page 168)

♥ **Children aged 3–6:** Stories 4 (page 54), 5 (page 66), 9 (page 104), 14 (page 164), 15 (page 167) and 16 (page 168)

♥ **Children aged 10–13:** Stories 10 (page 116), 17 (page 178), 18 (page 190) and 19 (page 213)

♥ **Single parent:** Stories 8 (page 94), 10 (page 116) and 19 (page 213)

♥ **Disharmonious relations with a partner:** Stories 8 (page 94), 10 (page 116) and 17 (page 178)

THREE

Anxiousness, nerviness, shyness

Around 40% of children are insecure. They may be clingy, scared to be in challenging situations or easily frightened by things that others of their age never worry about. They may express the insecurity by adopting an aloof position, avoiding emotion in themselves and others, although from time to time they collapse and parents can see how scared they are deep down. Or they may be a confusing mixture of clinginess and aloofness: sometimes one, sometimes the other.

Such children have developed a heightened sensitivity to threat, particularly the threat of feeling unloved or abandoned or rejected. Deep down, they just want to be cuddled, to be made to feel safe. For a baby, the greatest threat is if there is no one there who is responding to his unique signals. For a toddler, the main threat is of being abandoned or rejected, as well as not being responded to. If that is their normal situation, they can feel permanently threatened throughout their early years.

When humans (or other mammals, like monkeys) are threatened, it activates a 'fight–flight' system. A chemical, cortisol, is secreted, and it prepares the person to take instant action either to escape or to eliminate the threat. A child who often has a feeling of being threatened by danger in early childhood develops an abnormal level of cortisol. In many cases, it can rise to high levels, with the result that the child is constantly imagining dangers all around, even when there are none. Stuff can be going on that seems innocuous to all the other children, but to the high-cortisol child it poses extreme risk: Will his parents remember to pick him up after school? Is that spider going to bite him? Will it be safe to go to sleep in a strange bedroom when, at age 10, staying at a friend's house?

Equally, a child who has felt constantly threatened when small can become so used to it that the system that switches on the cortisol response becomes inactive. The child is blunted to danger: almost nothing triggers secretion of cortisol. In later life, they could be someone who will stay outwardly calm even if a mad axe-man bursts suddenly into a room.

Anxious, nervy, clingy children often respond extremely well to Love Bombing. Their distressed state means they have occasional temper tantrums, which usually disappear after LB, too. The feeling of being loved and of being in control resets their cortisol levels. But, equally importantly, the parents frequently realize just how vulnerable their child has been feeling and are able to take special care afterwards to make him feel safe and more independent.

STORY 4

Two awaydays
Fear of separation from mother: Sam, aged 3

Emma has two children, Sam, aged 3, and Jimmy, aged 2. For practical reasons, she wasn't able to go away for the night, so

instead she did LB with Sam for one day each on two con-
secutive weekends. She has a supportive husband.

Sam's problems

Sam seemed a lot more sensitive than his younger brother. He
was easily overwhelmed by simple situations that would not pose
a problem to most children of his age. Sometimes he would melt
down in rages more commonly seen in toddlers. But his most
obvious difficulty was that he got very jumpy when separated
from Emma. 'In the house, he wants to know where I am all
the time', she said.

For example, one afternoon she had told him they were going
to be hanging out at home. When she went upstairs, he started
shouting 'Mum, where are you? I need to know where you are!'
She shouted down to say where she was, but he was so busy
yelling 'I can't hear you. Where are you? I need to know' that he
could not hear her reply.

Sam has been at a very child-centred nursery since he was
2½, but he still had quite a few days when he did not want to
go. His nervousness showed up in the fact that he would not go
on outings with the other children, even if they were taken by
parents of children he knew. On such days, Emma would have
to pick him up early.

For much of the time Emma felt that Sam was a happy,
well-balanced 3-year-old. By no means were the difficulties she
described signs of some rare, sinister illness. At least a third of
children of this age have similar troubles. But Emma wanted to
understand why Sam was so nervous and to do something to
help him to be calmer and more secure.

Love Bombing

Preparing for the LB

Before the day, she asked him what he would like to do and if he could think of a name for the time they would spend together. He called it Pirate Day after a pirate ship on Adventure Island, a play centre in their town. Whenever they have driven past it, he has said, 'I will go on that one day, Mummy.' As it turned out, the idea of going on the ship was more important than actually doing it. As Emma reported, 'The funny thing is that he didn't actually like it when we did, but he still says, "I went on that, Mummy" when we go past. So it was a really big thing.'

The first LB Saturday

As planned, they did all his favourite things, notably the big funfair and Adventure Island. Emma got him a permit allowing access to the rides. In the event, he did not like any of them, but, Emma says, 'The point was, he could have gone on them if he'd wanted to. What he did like was the crazy golf and going to the aquarium to look at the fish.'

When they went to see a film about pirates, Sam did not like it. Normally, Emma would have said, 'We've come in, so why not stay for a bit and just try it?', but because it was Sam's day and he said, 'I don't like it, can we go straight away?', that's what they did. Emma comments that 'It was really good for me, actually, to say "yes" to everything. That made me realize how much I have got into a pattern of endless negotiation. It was really liberating for both of us. He wanted to have a go on one of those cars that you drive yourself. Of course, he couldn't steer it in any shape or form, he just kept driving into the wall. But I didn't make him get off, he could just carry on crashing it as much as he liked, and it was really a lot of fun for him.'

She didn't have to tell him off at all the whole day, and 'It was brilliant, he really responded to it.' They had a slush-puppy, and toast and a banana milkshake in a 1950s-style café that he really liked. For lunch he had a burger and chips, and he started banging the plates a bit. Normally that would have panicked Emma and she would have said, 'Stop that or we'll have to go home!', but because it was his day, she just said, 'Can you stop banging the plates?' and he did. To Emma, that was 'Quite astounding, really.'

She repeatedly told Sam that she loved him. When they started, she made a point of looking at her watch every 15 minutes or so and then telling him. Once into the habit, she just continued. Emma says that since then it has become a lot easier to tell him, and he says it back. She believes they now have 'much, much better communication. It was good fun, a great day that reminded us of the good times that we can have together, setting us back on that track. It was a truly lovely day.'

Emma wishes she could have done the whole weekend, saying 'Hopefully we will when my youngest is a bit older, because I didn't want the day to end, it would have been good to carry on.'

The half-hour evening Top-Ups

The following week she managed to organize nightly half-hour Top-Ups. They had bought a soft toy at the aquarium, a Kelpie sea horse, as his memento. Emma says, 'It's been very helpful for the Top-Ups. We will get my youngest off to sleep, then play some games, do a jigsaw. To begin with we called it Pirate Day Time, and then it turned into Magic Time. That can be Magic Daddy Time if the little one isn't sleeping, or Magic Mummy if he is. He's quite happy to transfer it across to his Daddy, maybe because he sees so little of him. That makes it even more special.

They tend to just sit quietly together, playing a game or watching TV. It's late in the evening, and they don't want anything too stimulating. If my husband does it, the sea horse helps to bring it back to Sam.'

The impact of the first LB day

There was an immediate improvement in Sam's willingness to be separated from Emma, which she attributes to the LB day.

The Pirate Day was on a Sunday. Monday was Sam's first ever concert at nursery, and he had been saying he didn't want to do it, and Emma told him, 'You don't have to if you don't want to.' She did not think he really believed her, but in the event, when they got there, he loved it. Emma was surprised: 'He was so wobbly, tearful, a very different Sam from the angry one. Normally he would just get really cross if he didn't want to do something. It was as if he could feel his feelings now, which was much easier for me and the teachers to deal with. So I left him with the teachers, who were brilliant, and said I would come back and that if he didn't want to do it, it didn't matter. But when I came back he was happy and he was fine, he did it. Amazing!'

On the Wednesday, 'a really big thing' was a trip to the fire station. The children were all going to go in parents' cars, but Sam did not want to go because it would be with someone else's Mum. Again, Emma said he didn't have to, or if he went and felt unhappy, they could ring her and she would come and pick him up. Once more, this worked: 'He did it. He would never have done that before the Pirate Day, he's always refused to go on any trips with the nursery before. He's never gone anywhere at all without me or his Dad, not anywhere, so that was a huge deal, massive.'

She also noticed that Sam was much more eager to enjoy her

company, rather than just clinging. They went swimming with both the boys. Neither can swim. Usually Sam takes himself off to the shallow end. This time he wanted to be with Emma: lots more physical contact, lots more playing with her.

Emma felt that the LB day had taught her different ways of handling Sam. She noticed her habit of setting him up with something, like breakfast or a game or a TV programme, and then going away and doing something else. On the Pirate Day she could not do that. So he came with her everywhere, to make the beds, to put her makeup on, to pack the bags – they stuck together like glue. There was none of the 'Mummy where are you'. She realized the extent to which she had tended to leave him and not explain where she was going. So now she will tell him even if she is going just into another room. The result is that he no longer screams out to ask where she is.

The second LB day

The next Saturday, Emma arranged a lot of things that would not cost money, like swimming, making cakes, playing games, and at first this was 'The Bad Day'. It was 'I don't want to make cakes now. Where is Daddy? Where is Jimmy? Where have they gone, can I go with them?' Emma would explain patiently that this was their special time, and Sam would say he did not want it. He wanted to be with Daddy. She remembered what I had told her about him trying to annoy her, that this might happen, so she decided not to storm off or to respond with 'Fine, then we'll go get Daddy.'

Eventually, she recalls, 'Sam did lose it, a real upset, off into this completely unreachable place, but he did let me hold him, just sitting on my lap yelling. I remembered when he was 6–8 months old he would scream like that for 20 minutes every day after my husband went to work: All smiles, "bye-bye,

Daddy", all lovely for him and then completely go bananas. He was exactly the same. This was for about 35 minutes, and I suddenly got through when I said, "Daddy really does love you, when he's not here he still cares about and misses you", and he did stop. And then we had a nice rest of the day.'

They made cakes, played games and had a pleasurable shared time.

The Top-Ups

Keeping the Magic Time up required a big effort. Her husband gets home at 7, so it is hard to find time to fit it in. Quite often Sam has fallen asleep before Dad gets home. It is hard to do it with her younger son still awake and without her husband, unless she splits it into two 15-minute sessions.

The impact of the second LB day

Emma reports that 'He has not had any unreachable tantrums since that one on the last LB day, four weeks ago, which is the biggest single thing of all: he can get calmer quicker, is never unreachable, much better at communicating what the problem is. He gets tearful, feels the upset and frustration now, instead of just mindless red mist, kicking and raging, panic-stricken. I think that panic would get through to me and I would panic too: "He's going to have another meltdown, I'm going to have to take him home, this is awful." Now I can say, "We'll find the missing toy" or look for it and if we can't find it we will just have to say "It's lost". And because he can really hear me now, that's okay, I can understand what he's upset about. We never developed that because we both panicked. I don't panic any more. This is the biggest and the best thing of all, a huge change.'

The impact of the LB as a whole, and the causes of Sam's problems

Emma believes that the LB changed her as well as Sam. She believes his fear of her disappearing can be traced back to very early in his life.

Emma's parents lived near her when Sam was born. During the pregnancy, her father suffered a stroke. Emma's mother was tremendously stretched in every way by this misfortune, which placed considerable stress on Emma. She found herself having to care for her father for two afternoons a week, to give her mother a break. Emma wryly commented that 'Some people's Mums help you with your newborn, but my Mum said, "Can you have your Dad?"'

Sam was one of those newborns who cried a lot for most of the day (this is true of about one quarter of babies, usually as a result of problems during the pregnancy or birth). Looking back, Emma feels she was particularly ill-equipped to cope because it had been exactly the same with her and her mother. 'She was unable to show me how to comfort him because she had not known how to comfort me', she told me.

The period after his birth, she recalls, 'was a bad time, I was quite depressed. My health visitor was not a particularly nice person, and she said at the time that I was keeping Sam in my bed for my own comfort and that I ought to get him out. She claimed there was only a small window of opportunity and otherwise I would never get him out. I was breastfeeding so much that I was really torn, because it was comforting him. But I cut it down at that time because of what she said, and that made it a really tough time for him, he lost everything. That was when I got into the habit of walking away from him because I didn't want him to see me crying in front of him, so I would set him up with food and snacks and games, going away to have a cry. I'd suffered a shock – my father's stroke and impending death – and, without meaning to, I created a loss for him.'

The 'controlled crying' that the health visitor recommended is highly controversial. On the one hand, there is strong evidence that it does unsettle babies and make them more prone to being insecure in later life. On the other, in some cases, it does lead to sleep patterns that fit in better with adult routines. For hard-pressed working mothers, it is easy to see that is attractive, and if it can be made to work – which it often does not – then it is understandable that it is used. It is also important to bear in mind that if the mother does not get enough sleep because the baby is constantly waking her, she is more likely to get depressed, also creating problems for the baby.

As the months passed, Sam calmed down, but when he was 9 months old Emma's father died. Bereft, she found it hard to stay cheerful. She was not suffering a clinical depression or anything as extreme as that, but – again with hindsight – she can see how things now became very hard for him. 'You just feel a bit funny when your parents die, don't you', she recalled. She was at pains to avoid Sam seeing her crying, so she kept suddenly disappearing. At other times she was not there emotionally: inexplicably so from Sam's viewpoint.

Alas, even worse was to come. Her husband is a civil servant who works extremely long hours, often having to attend meetings in the evening. When Sam was 15 months old, his father was transferred almost to the other end of England, a place where they knew no one and to which they had to move. It took them two years to sell their house, resulting in three moves during that period because they were renting. 'When we moved, Sam lost the house that he was used to, my Mum and the people we knew: we didn't know a soul here. On top of that, when my father died, in a way Sam lost me, because I couldn't really give him the attention and responsiveness he needed.'

Emma felt that Sam's nervousness about being separated from her was a legacy of these difficult changes in his life, combined with his shaky early years. Interestingly, there is good evidence that frequent house moves do increase the risk of distress in children.

As a result of the LB, Emma has changed the way she acts. She sticks closer to Sam rather than wanting to get away and do things. She is no longer thinking 'Where did that come from? We were having a nice day, why has he gone bananas?', because she is with him more and can see the precursors to his distress. She says 'yes' to him 'ever so much more'. She used to feel that as a parent it would be bad to do that, and now she thinks, 'What the hell?' She believes that parents of toddlers can create a stick to beat themselves with by not distinguishing the real No-Nos (like running across the road) from the unimportant ones. Being much more relaxed, she says, 'We have much more "I love you, Daddy loves you, we're proud of you."'

At the same time, it is possible that the LB and Top-Up periods have, in themselves, helped to reset Sam's emotional thermostat. The key may have been for him to revisit the specific distress of being left alone with a downcast mother by his father, except that, this time, it was alright. He may now able to believe that his mother is not downcast and to grasp that his father's departure is not a rejection. She has become someone he can depend upon.

Emma gave an example of how the dynamic has changed: 'I shouted at him yesterday when he soaked me with the hosepipe – stupid, give a 3-year-old a hose, and of course he's going to cover you with water. I said, "Don't wet me, just do the grass." Then I got cross, and he said, "Tell me I'm a good boy, be my friend, you are proud of me, really." He made me feel awful. I said, "You're right, I am proud of you, I shouldn't have given you that hosepipe!"' He felt confident enough to say this and had faith that she would listen. She was able to hear him and set matters right.

Quite often Sam comes and sleeps in their bed, close to her. She believes that this, combined with her staying closer to him when they are together, is the basis of his greater separateness: 'In the daytime he can go and play away independently, it's quite amazing. By having felt dependent, he can be independent.'

There has also been a change in the way her husband relates to the family. She says, 'My husband, obviously, is a lot happier. I don't force him to go on stressful family days any more; he will take Jimmy out, and Sam and I will have a quiet morning in. I don't know why we didn't think of it earlier. On a family day, my husband's trying to talk to me, I'm trying to talk to the children, and they're trying to talk to their father. It's just a nightmare. Whereas if everybody comes back and has some special time, my husband feels really confident now with the children. He came back the other day after a morning with Sam and said, "I can't remember when I've had so much fun."'

She believes that one-on-one with each child is an obvious way to remember how lovable and amusing they are: 'You can forget in the busyness of the routine. I'd recommend it to anybody. You see it as mandatory for couples – go away for the weekend, have some special time, a date – why not the same with children?'

Postscript

Nearly a year after Sam's LB, I received the following email from Emma.

Just to let you know, we are still on the 'programme' with Sam, except, due to work commitments, Sam's Dad couldn't do the 'man time' at bedtime they had been doing together. We didn't notice anything different at first, but then after a couple of weeks or so, we could really notice a difference in Sam's demeanour, nothing huge as in the past, just a bit less listening to us, needing to be asked three or four or five times to do something, and certainly more emotional. As in, crying at little things, becoming more angry or upset quicker, and for longer. So, as current conditions still stop us from a full-on 'lovebombing' weekend, I just took Sam out of nursery on Friday morning, at the same time as his brother now goes.

We had a lovely time, very slow and quiet, surprisingly. Sam wanted a milkshake and teacake at a local cafe and took about an hour to eat it. Then we got a *Scooby Doo* DVD from the library and watched it at home with some popcorn. I was really good and resisted using my mobile or popping on the computer or any of the hundred-and-one impulses I got to do things whilst this was going on. The results are great. A small meltdown in the afternoon after we picked up his brother, which is understandable, and then just back to normal good, sweet, loving, silly and a bit naughty behaviour. The one-to-one time is like a little reset button. I think it's good for both of us, as it stops me from always being on the go and slows me down too.

Thanks again for your help, I can honestly say Sam is like a different boy and it has helped in how I relate to my younger son, as well as creating a family dynamic whereby my husband will take one child out on their own with him every weekend. It works a treat for us all.

STORY 5

One night away
Scared of groups, scared of losing toys: Gina, aged 3

Gina, 3, has a sister who is 18 months younger than she. Her mother Jo is a highly competent, conscientious woman. She has a supportive partner.

Her initial email read as follows:

> Hello, regretfully I followed a book when my now 3-year-old daughter was born. While I didn't follow it to the letter and took what I felt was a middle way, there were times when I did bits of controlled crying. She is now at times anxious, particularly about losing things that float or fly (like a balloon), as if she needs to feel in control of things.
>
> I feel very guilty that it could be partly attributed to her experience in earlier life. She has also received an enormous amount of love throughout her life and continues to do so. Can I do anything to help her with her anxiety?

Gina's problems

Gina would get exceptionally upset if she was likely to lose something and was prone to severe tantrums. Balls that could roll away from her, balloons that could fly away, they upset her a lot. She would be beside herself.

She was also shy. In larger groups she would not join in, like when singing at nursery she would just want to sit on Jo's knee. She was quite serious, a bit moody, preoccupied. Perhaps most worrying of all in a child of that age, Gina could not let go and enjoy herself.

Planning the LB

Talking it over with Gina, they decided to spend a night in a rented caravan in the countryside. Jo showed Gina pictures of it and the lovely surrounding countryside. Gina chose how they would get there, what they would do. She was looking forward to making a fire and cooking on it. She chose the books they would read. With such a small child, there was a limit to how many of the decisions could be made by her, but Jo tried to involve her as much as possible. Gina called it their 'caravan weekend'.

The LB weekend

The Saturday

They set off on the Saturday morning by train. They spent some of the day in a beautiful city nearby before going to the caravan. Gina had a strong sense of an adventure and enjoyed having a meal in the city. Around teatime they got the bus to near the place where the caravan was and were picked up by the farmer who owns it. Having settled in, they lit a fire and cooked sausages and marshmallows. Then they lay in a hammock, and Jo read stories from the books Gina had chosen. They settled in the double bed and, having played and cuddled, had a good night's sleep.

The Sunday

After playing around in the countryside and looking at the farm, they got the bus back to the city. They went to the cathedral and watched the choir. Gina was awestruck by the atmosphere, the children in the choir singing, the huge nave, the spectacular stained-glass windows. The sights and sounds sent Gina into a joyful state. They visited the city's castle and were also impressed by the size and age of the surroundings. They spent about two hours in an ice-cream parlour, with Gina rejoicing in the freedom and attention.

Gina was quite reluctant to enter into the 'telling her I love her' component of the weekend. Instead, Jo concentrated on speaking about why Gina was special to her, what attributes she loved, what was lovely about her, but mostly just the fact of her existence.

Because Jo had been swamped by the job of caring for two small children for three years, it was also a chance for her to reflect on the way she mothered.

The Top-Ups

On their return, Jo struggled to keep the Top-Ups going. Instead, she says that 'I have completely changed my approach to looking after Gina. I read a book called *Unconditional Parenting*, by Alfie Kohn, about avoiding reward and punishment as the way to control children. I've tried to be more compassionate, so that when Gina has the tantrums, I just try and support her through it. My Mum used to get furious with me when I was angry and I used to do that. Now, if Gina can't have something, I have given her a cuddle and talked to her about it.' Thus, instead of Top-Ups, Jo has changed the way she relates to Gina at all times, as much as possible.

The effect of the LB

Jo says, 'That weekend was brilliant as the beginning of a new way of going on between us, a springboard for me to change my approach. Over time, we have built up trust between us. When she was smaller, I think my love was too conditional on her obeying me. If she was screaming her head off about something tiny, it was too much for me to deal with at times. Because I had two kids very close together I have been pretty exhausted for a couple of years. The little one has been a terrible sleeper, and you are not the most patient when you are exhausted.'

The effect on Gina's personality and behaviour has been profound, if gradual and not total. According to Jo, 'She has become less anxious. She felt special and felt loved during the LB. I was not expecting her to change overnight, and it was a gradual process of change, as I altered the way I reacted when she got anxious. Over the weekend she felt in control. It was also a period when I had a little chance to reflect and think, which I had not had, and that was of real value. I will do an LB weekend again, I don't see it as a one-off. My husband is going to do it with the younger one. We've bought a little caravan so we can do it with both of them.'

Regarding the changes in Gina, Jo notices that 'She is less worried about losing things or things leaving her. She feels a bit more solid. She's not an entirely different girl, she is still shy in big groups, won't take part straight away. But she's settled into nursery, and she very much takes part, which she didn't early on. She's got some good friends that she does feel secure with. At home, she's now generally fine, the tantrums have ended. She's a bit of a perfectionist and gets a bit cross if she can't get a puzzle quite right.'

The causes of Gina's problems

Jo comments: 'I've done a lot of reflection in the last year about how I looked after her and what I can do to make her feel more secure. She was 18 months old when her sister Samantha was born. It meant Gina sometimes had to wait, because Samantha came first. I feel like she's had a bit of a hard time, I wouldn't do the same again. I don't feel I've been an awful Mum, they have had a pretty good deal, but there's things you could have done differently. I'm living and I'm learning.'

She believes she was misguided in the earliest years with Gina. 'When you've got a first baby you don't realize how sensitive they are. She was quite an easy baby and she didn't scream her head off, but I tried to instil a routine. If an educated woman like me can read up on all the books and still make the wrong decision, not questioning what I was being told, what chance does an uneducated person have? Perhaps being a policewoman by profession made me more strict as a parent. On reflection, letting her scream at all was not good for her security. But you never know, she might have been a slightly anxious child whatever I did. It was quite a stressful pregnancy, because I was working full-time, and a nightmare birth.'

To a certain extent, Gina's problems could be regarded as being caused by excessive modern expectations of what small children can cope with when young. Jo believes that 'Children don't really like large groups. They go too early. She didn't go to nursery till she was 3. I would be keen to keep her out 'til 6 or 7. She wants to be like other children, wouldn't want to miss out. But she finds it incredibly stressful when there's over 100 kids in the playground. The whole thing is so exposing.'

Part of Jo's difficulties in relating to Gina arose from her own experience with her mother. 'She was really harsh, although she also did give me a lot of love. I remember it so clearly, my Mum blanking me. My Dad would come and give me a hug. I need to forgive my Mum.' Through LB and adoption of Alfie Kohn's *Unconditional Love* parenting approach, Jo intends to give Gina a different experience from her own.

WHERE TO GO NEXT IN THE BOOK

Other LB stories that relate to this chapter:

- ♥ **Two nights away:** Stories 1 (page 27), 2 (page 37), 6 (page 73), 11 (page 126), 17 (page 178) and 18 (page 190)

- ♥ **One night away:** Stories 3 (page 44), 7 (page 86), 8 (page 94) and 20 (page 216)

- ♥ **Awaydays:** Stories 9 (page 104) and 19 (page 213)

- ♥ **At home:** Stories 10 (page 116), 12 (page 156), 13 (page 162), 14 (page 164), 15 (page 167) and 16 (page 168)

- ♥ **Spending little or no money:** Stories 8 (page 94), 9 (page 104), 10 (page 116), 12 (page 156), 13 (page 162), 14 (page 164), 15 (page 167) and 16 (page 168)

- ♥ **Children aged 3–6:** Stories 2 (page 37), 3 (page 44), 9 (page 104), 14 (page 164), 15 (page 167) and 16 (page 168)

- ♥ **Single parent:** Stories 1 (page 27), 8 (page 94), 10 (page 116) and 19 (page 213)

FOUR

Self-loathing, wanting to die

Children with negative thoughts about themselves are especially upsetting to meet, not to mention that, as parents, it breaks our hearts if we hear our child say things like 'I'm an idiot', 'No wonder everyone hates me, I'm horrible', 'I'm just a hopeless person'. Alas, we live in societies that make this all too common. The pressure to succeed with peers, to be popular, has never been greater. The means for achieving this – be it exam success, looking good, sporting prowess – so easily become vehicles for misery rather than the outlets for pleasure and satisfaction that they could be.

Of course, thank goodness, most children are spared these feelings before puberty, although horrifyingly high proportions suffer them in adolescence, especially girls. A host of things can go wrong in families and make a child more vulnerable. Feeling unloved when a sibling comes along, becoming the victim of bullying at school, neglect or hostility during the early years, feeling over-controlled by zealous parents: there are all sorts of possibilities. But perhaps the commonest is witnessing parental disharmony. Children are very prone to blame themselves if parents row a lot, and the example in this chapter illustrates how effective Love Bombing can be in reversing that misery.

STORY 6

Two nights away
Self-loathing, meltdowns: Tim, aged 9

Tim, aged 9, has a sophisticated, clever, 12-year-old sister, Tanya, and a much younger brother, Gerry, aged 2. His mother, Marianne, is a hard-working, successful professional, as is his Dad, John.

In this case, over a two-year period I received reports on progress from Marianne, as well as some reports from Tim himself.

Tim's problems

Marianne's initial email to me set out the situation with some clarity.

> I am writing for perhaps some brief but pertinent advice with regard to my 9-year-old son. He's lovely, incredibly sweet and charming but seems to not like himself and has no focus. He has a 12-year-old, academically capable, sister – also very capable at knowing how to wind him up. We sometimes don't even notice what she's done, only his extreme over-reaction, which is becoming increasingly violent. He also has a 2-year-old brother whose arrival deeply undermined Tim's position as the youngest and only boy. Although Tim does love him, the little one is rather nervous of what Tim might do next.
>
> I'm afraid that I am in the process of F***ing him up. Tim constantly says that he hates himself, wants to die, he's rubbish at everything, and I don't know how to 'turn this off'!

He is as bright as his sister but doesn't believe that he is, explodes at the mention of homework and reacts negatively to most suggestions.

I'm not at my tether's end yet, but I don't want to wait until I get there. I'm worried that I will have an unruly and unhappy teenager that I cannot help later on. I largely agree with you that the nurture parameter is the far more powerful one, but we can't see what we're doing wrong at the moment. We do both work full-time (and the rest), particularly for the past year or so, when work has been demanding.

Marianne was not despairing, but she felt unsure how she could manage matters so that Tim would move into a less negative and aggressive state. She continued as follows:

I can vaguely see how one might change a child's view of the world and himself. It's also easy to see from Tim that when he receives individual attention, his behaviour (which I probably make sound worse than it actually is) improves drastically. It's seeing how we can fit it into an "Affluenza" world [*this is a reference to a book I had written suggesting that we have become overly concerned with the pursuit of money, possessions, appearances and fame*]. I don't mean that we are obsessed with the pursuit of wealth, but we have no choice but to work the hours that we do, at the expense of time with the children. In the same way your father believed in you and your education, we would like to do the same for our kids. I don't believe that your parents' investment has been wasted!

Tim saw my initial email to you and seemed rather pleased about it. My email to you today coincides with the imminent death of my father: he is very "poorly" (the word the doctors are using, would you believe!). It is making us consider how we're handling our lives and the time we spend with each other and the children. This is no surprise, I suppose. As my father leaves, it is memories of time spent with him (and it's the better times rather than the difficult ones that come to mind) that are resonating now. So, for Tim – and for Tanya and Gerry – I would like to give better tools for life and good experiences to fall back on.

The Love Bombing

Since she and her husband were affluent professionals, Marianne could easily afford to take Tim away for a weekend at a hotel. This is her account of the experience, one week later:

> We were both a bit nervous before leaving on Friday evening. Tim had intimated to our nanny that he wasn't sure what we would do together, and I was wondering whether I should take a book or not! When we arrived at the hotel, Tim thought it was the best place ever (we asked for a chocolate fountain in our room!) and we went out for dinner together. Tim tried food he wouldn't normally try (mussels on Saturday! spat them out, but he still tried). We watched TV after dinner and on the Saturday began the 'Can I have this?'. I had thought about trying to call you and ask as to the exact extent of saying yes to everything but decided to just go with the flow.
>
> It started with wanting three pairs of sunglasses (a fiver each only) from a very odd shop (Halloween stuff/people into S&M, maybe fancy dress) that Tim declared was the best shop ever. It was followed by wanting sweets, but, for a sweetie addict, nowhere near as much as I expected: if anything, it was decidedly less than he would usually have at the weekend. We then went clothes shopping for Tim, and whilst he probably selected more items than

he normally would have done, they were all great and he needed some new tops anyway. I did want to get some things for the other children. When I mentioned that in fact this was his weekend, he latched onto that and didn't really want me to look for a coat for Tanya. I did concede. We went for lunch, after which I was tired, but he wanted to go to the Oceanarium, which I think I enjoyed more than any of the other kids there! It was great fun, and we bought all kinds of rubbish in the gift shop (this time, for his siblings too).

It made Tim feel very special; it definitely worked. It was better us going away rather than staying at home and the others going off. I realize not everyone could afford that. To be honest, he was reasonable about absolutely everything. You could see him setting himself limits, 'I don't need this extra one'.

There was more shopping and walking around. I had thought that Tim would enjoy walking along the beach, but we have different ideas about how to enjoy it. I realized that I like just walking on the sand, but it's no fun for Tim if he's not in a swimsuit making sandcastles. Curiously, he didn't want to try anything that seemed dangerous. There's a stationary hot-air balloon and one of those bungee-jumping things, but neither was of interest to him.

I think I finally only hinted that some self-control was needed when we were in a shop where *Warhammer* games can be quite expensive, so Tim was moderate in his choice there! We had been walking around from 10 a.m. to 5 p.m.

We went back to the hotel and got some KFC, watched *The X Factor* and went to bed quite late. On Sunday we pottered around again, did some shopping and decided to go to a zoo on the way back. We got a bit lost (our sat nav decided not to help us), but after that Tim was quite keen to come home.

Tim spent a great deal of time cuddling up to me and telling me how much he loved me (always reciprocated). It was interesting for me not to be in charge. I'm not terribly dictatorial if I take the others out, but I do tend to lead or move them onto the next thing. Here, it really was mostly Tim's decision what we did next, what we ate, what we watched and what he bought. Even with the clothes, I would normally tend to guide him, and this time I didn't unless he asked, and, rather than making him choose, we got all the ones he liked.

The Top-Ups

Marianne found the Top-Up hard to implement. If she was home on time, then there was a lot to do; if late, it was too close to their bedtime and she felt too tired. In the first week, they compromised with 15 minutes on the Thursday and not at all on the Friday.

The short-term effect of the LB: 1 week later

Marianne reported that 'The truth is, both Tim and I loved the experience. I really loved spending time with him and getting to know him. Oddly enough, we both seem to "hear" each other better: I mean, I don't have to repeat myself as often and I am more attuned to his requests. So far we haven't had any major unhappiness from Tim.' He has had one explosion since the weekend, when Marianne asked him to do his homework, but it was much milder than usual. Marianne records that 'There was no self-loathing (just doesn't want to do the homework), and I stayed calm, so the whole thing passed very quickly. Although he's still being very annoying about homework, he hasn't directed that at himself, and it seems mostly a "controlled explosion". Let's see!!!'

Marianne also noticed that 'Once you have more than one child, you never spend that much time alone with each of them. It's an extraordinary thought that your children will rarely get that much of you until they're an adult! It is obvious, I guess, but the oddness of it had never struck me before. I really enjoyed Tim's company once I had released the thought that we need to discuss the "important" things: his behaviour and his attitude to homework (mostly the 11+ stuff I'm making him do).'

The effect 5 weeks after the LB

Marianne sent me an update:

The Love Bombing weekend was great, but I was not very good at providing the half-hour a night that you suggested. I think that by definition, the mother who 'causes' the requirement for Love Bombing her 10-year-old cannot give him her undivided attention for half an hour every day even if it is just for two weeks, and especially not in a recession and with two other kids and having taken him away, creating a new level of jealousy with his sister! I give Tim random bits of time and have recently taken to holding and cuddling him like a baby and even saying to him, "You're my baby boy and I love you." He's small for his age, which he's unhappy about, but he still very cute to cuddle. Whereas Gerry, the 2-year-old, would and does say, "I not a baby", Tim completely soaks it up, and for the 5 minutes he's being held in this way he seems to revert a bit. Tanya has taken to gate-crashing our half-hour LB sessions, and they always turn into something else.

I would say that, overall, Tim is happier. He still has tantrums, but since the weekend away I haven't heard him say that he hates himself at all: not once, come to think of it. He seems gentler and less aggressively playful with Gerry, but not always, and still resists doing homework with me. He says I stress him when I ask him to do it. He also still loses it occasionally, but the tantrum doesn't last as long and is not so full of hatred.

I am concerned that the further in time we move away from the LB weekend, the more he might revert to previous behaviour. Not to mention that Tanya is getting quite jealous and so has started to return to bossing him a bit (the LB weekend also helped her be nicer to him for a while, for some reason: they get on famously well when they do and infamously badly when they don't).

So what is it that has to change on a day-to-day basis? I don't know really. We still have 'cuddles': the three of us tend to either watch a film together or they come to my bed for a chat. Tanya can dominate the conversation at these times, and if I ask her to give Tim a chance she gets upset and says I love him more than her.

Actually, if I think about the whole thing, his avoidance of homework and his strange sudden squeals or loud noises are the bones of contention now, and occasionally winding up Gerry. In fact, I'm probably less worried about him than I was when I first wrote to you. In fact, I've just realized that he really is happier! It's how to maintain it, and apply it across the board to the rest of his life.

The effect 18 months later

In the time after that email, Tim had passed some very exacting exams. Marianne was quite jubilant about his progress, much of which she attributed to the LB and the associated changes in their family. She wrote as follows:

It is getting better, really, and it is largely due to the LB and subsequent changes. I really was at a loss and couldn't see the trees for the woods, or some such! We are going back to family 'cuddles', and I do give Tim more time. I am changing back to where we were before I started working 70 hours a week. It is getting better, and he is getting a great deal more time from me than before.

Looking back, there were four things which could have meant I did not tune in to Tim, with disastrous results: my business was under tremendous pressure, so I had to work incredibly hard; my father died; Tim wanted to get good exam results but was not willing to put in the hours; and we moved house. Mostly, I wanted to thank you for improving our lives, because without the awareness you raised about my relationship with Tim it could have been quite awful.

Although we managed the half-hour together only occasionally, we did spend more time chatting, and I check my irritation at the constant noise and hyperactivity that seems to be the way boys grow! We have a lot more cuddles, and even when I ask him to stop tapping/fidgeting/jumping off sofas/screeching etc., it's done in a better spirit and with less 'stressiness'. More importantly, he hasn't screamed like a banshee for ages, I don't believe he's said he hates himself and wants to die at all (maybe once or twice), and he hasn't tried to kill his sister, though he's still not too thrilled with the privileges (and sometimes existence) of his younger brother.

He recently turned 11, and all the awful entrance exams are over. He got into his preferred school by the skin of his teeth (I don't really know how, because he really didn't do much work for it).

All this after just a weekend away together and a bit of awareness! Just think if I actually had given him the half-hour a day that you suggested!

Tim's account of the LB

An able and thoughtful boy, Tim told Marianne that he wanted to explain what it had been like from his standpoint. This is what he sent me:

> Dear Oliver (This is Tim),
>
> I had a really, really, really etc. good time with my Mum that weekend and thank you so much for the idea. I think I spend a lot more good time with my Mum now.
>
> As you know, me and my Mum went to a hotel and we had soooooooo much chocolate (and it was goooood.)
>
> My Mum spoilt me rotten. I had so much fun and I've told all my friends about you and the hotel and how it's such a good idea. My Mum spent almost £600 on me!
>
> I hope you are well.
>
> Best wishes!
>
> Tim
>
> (I may email again soon. Bye!)

I replied, asking him how important the spending of money had been in the weekend away. This was his analysis.

> Dear OJ (This is Tim),
>
> The weekend away made me know that my Mum was always loving and caring for me (not that I didn't know). As

a result my Mum feels that she would like to spend more time with me.

I don't think spending money is the best thing of going on this trip because the point of it is that you need to spend time with your Mum or Dad and get to know them more and not just to spend money. So the best bit of the Love Bombing was just being with my Mum alone with no one else to care about.

Me and my Mum used to argue a bit because we didn't really (if you know what I mean) know each other as well as we should and this made me anxious to spend time with her. We don't argue as much and I feel that my Mum is happier with me. I'm less angry with people in general.

Best wishes,
Tim

The causes of Tim's problems

Neither Tim nor Tanya slept well when small, to such an extent that when he was 9 months old they consulted a sleep 'expert' who persuaded Marianne to leave both children screaming in their rooms for three nights.

Although Marianne worked hard during the early years of all her children, the substitute care each had was different. Tanya and Gerry had highly responsive nannies, but this was not the case for Tim.

Marianne says that 'With Tim, I went back to work when he was 4 weeks old. The first nanny was not good. I came home on a hot day at lunchtime and he was swaddled in a hot rug, sitting on the front seat in the car. The nanny said, "This is very inconvenient for me: can't you stop interfering?"'

At 3 months, we had a very nice lady from the Congo for

a week who said, 'I don't understand about this milk, he needs some chicken.' She didn't seem to have noticed that he lacked any teeth! So I registered him for nursery but that was not great, so I moved him to the one where his sister was as soon as I could, but that was not until he was 2.'

Marianne also believes Tim felt very humiliated by his older sister, which she was adept at doing. When his younger brother arrived, the rivalry was increased.

It seems likely that the neglectful early care made him feel unvalued, which was made worse by subsequent rivalry. However, Marianne also believes that the pressures on her during his middle childhood meant she was not tuning in to him and that the LB not only helped to reset the emotional thermostat setting from his early years, it also enabled her to get on his wavelength from age 9.

WHERE TO GO NEXT IN THE BOOK

Other LB stories that relate to this chapter:

- ♥ **Two nights away:** Stories 1 (page 27), 2 (page 37), 11 (page 126), 17 (page 178) and 18 (page 190)

- ♥ **One night away:** Stories 3 (page 44), 5 (page 66), 7 (page 86), 8 (page 94) and 20 (page 216)

- ♥ **Awaydays:** Stories 4 (page 54), 9 (page 104) and 19 (page 213)

- ♥ **At home:** Stories 10 (page 116), 12 (page 156), 13 (page 162), 14 (page 164), 15 (page 167) and 16 (page 168)

- ♥ **Spending little or no money:** Stories 8 (page 94), 9 (page 104), 10 (page 116), 12 (page 156), 13 (page 162), 14 (page 164), 15 (page 167) and 16 (page 168)

♥ **Children aged 7–9:** Stories 7 (page 86), 8 (page 94), 11 (page 126), 12 (page 156), 13 (page 162), 14 (page 164) and 20 (page 216)

♥ **Single parent:** Stories 1 (page 27), 8 (page 94), 10 (page 116) and 19 (page 213)

FIVE

Sleep problems

Sleep problems are very common. At least one third of over-3-year-olds either have trouble getting to sleep alone or wake during the night and become fearful, or both. Not surprisingly, as a result they are tired during the day, making them more likely to be badly behaved and not enjoy themselves.

Some children cannot sleep because they are plagued by fears: they are going to be murdered in their beds, strangers are going to break in and kidnap them, monsters are all around, scratching at the window or hiding under the bed. Mostly, these children are insecure for the kinds of reasons described at the beginning of Chapter Three: they did not feel loved and safe when small, and this is dogging them at night.

Others are troubled by a bad conscience. Even though they may be perfectly behaved all day long, at night they are nagged by a sense of their wickedness or slothfulness or imperfection. For those who have been causing mayhem during the day, hitting others, acting with malice, creating chaos in their families, their guilty conscience keeps them awake.

Whatever the immediate reason for the wakefulness, in many cases Love Bombing seems to help a lot. The example in this chapter is an extreme case and is reassuring: given time and the right kind of support, almost any child can be helped to sleep peacefully.

STORY 7

One night away
Waking 25 times a night: Jess, aged 8

Jess, 8, had a younger sister aged 5. Her parents, Bill and Marion, worked full-time from early on in their children's lives.

I have stayed in touch with Jess's parents, and it is now five years since Marion did the LB, so the long-term impact of it can be evaluated.

Jess's problems

Aged 8, Jess was waking up some 25 times a night, even more often than a difficult baby. Bill and Marion were absolutely desperate, having tried all the tricks in all the books.

Jess would have difficulty in settling in her bed to go to sleep, although she was sharing a room with her younger sister. After eventually dropping off, she would wake up with a start and run into her parents' room in a panic. She told her mother that 'Sometimes I have nightmares, sometimes I just wake up and feel a bit scared.'

The problem had begun when Jess was 5. Hoping to solve it, her parents put her in the same room as her sister, so she did not feel alone. 'I need to be with somebody, to feel safe', she said. But it did not work: apparently this was not the 'somebody' she needed.

Sometimes her insecurities were also present during the day. Overall, Marion felt she was a 'very kind, a very good girl, not a naughty one, along the straight and narrow'. However, specifically when at home, she was terrified of being alone. Marion could 'see the fear in her eyes sometimes'. For example, she refused to go the lavatory alone, needing an adult to accompany her, leaving the door ajar and wanting to be reassured that they were waiting for her just outside. Even if her family were around, she would not go upstairs on her own. Yet, rather puzzlingly, she was perfectly happy to go on play dates, away from her family, able then to go to the lavatory unaccompanied. She was also perfectly happy going to school.

Her parents felt that Jess was excessively timid. She was easily worried if bad things happened to other people, like if they had an accident and broke an arm, taking it to heart.

Jess's new regime

Because they were so desperate for immediate help, I suggested that Jess sleep in her parents' bed and that they put her to sleep later than her sister, giving her some time just to be with them. This was introduced before they tried an LB weekend. It seemed the most practical way for everyone to start getting some sleep. Both parents were so exhausted they were grateful for any scheme that might achieve it. Whilst some experts strongly object to co-sleeping (as having a child in the parental bed is called), claiming that it only serves to create a bad habit and discourages the child from learning to cope on his own, there is potent evidence that it can be extremely reassuring to babies, toddlers, and older children too. Since it is very widely practised throughout the developing world, it is arguably a natural way of behaving and not dangerous.

The co-sleeping

Coming in the week before the LB weekend, co-sleeping quickly produced benefits. Marion and Bill took it in turns to do the job of staying with Jess in their bed until she fell asleep. She was able to do so from the first night, and she did not usually wake before they came upstairs. Bill, for example, would then sleep with her, and Marion would go into the spare room; if Jess needed the lavatory in the night, she would wake Bill but was able to go on her own, without him standing outside. Sometimes she slept through, and the number of interruptions quickly became fewer.

Whilst it was obviously tiresome for the parents to be parted, they were tremendously relieved to be getting a proper night's sleep. Equally gratifying, Jess was noticeably more open in talking about her time when away from them. Where they used to have to probe at length to get any information about her school day, now she was much more bubbly and forthcoming.

The downside was that her parents' evening was eaten into. They would take her up at around 8 o'clock, but it might be an hour before Jess fell asleep. She was now willing to go upstairs and to the lavatory on her own, but only in the evenings.

The LB weekend

Jess wanted to be taken to a zoo for the day by her mother, then to a nice hotel (they could just about afford such extravagances). She wanted them both to dress up for a special dinner together and then to mooch about the following day, relaxing in the hotel swimming pool.

All of these hopes were fulfilled. On return, Jess described it as 'the best weekend of my life'.

The evening Top-Ups

To begin with, it annoyed Bill that Jess often wanted them 'to watch the Disney channel or trash like *High School Musical*' with her. However, they gradually managed to persuade her to do more 'interactive' things, like playing board games. Eventually, she only wanted to spend the time in front of the TV for about half the evenings.

The longer-term outcome

As the months went by, Jess tended to want her father to be the one to get her to bed and to sleep with her. Perhaps because one of the original traumas had been depression in her mother (as discussed below), she felt safest with him.

After three months Jess was able to go upstairs to her room on her own when she was tired, following 'Mummy Time'. At first, she would read to herself after getting into bed and needed one of them to come and say goodnight. However, this quickly disappeared, and after a month, when they came up to check how she was, she would be asleep. At last they had got their evenings back, as well as their nights.

In a recent email to me five years after the LB, Bill wrote the following:

> Jess is very much now a teenager and, to be fair, is sleeping very well. She has no hang-ups about going to bed (other than wanting to stay on the iPad longer or BBM her mates!). She has regular sleepovers at people's houses, and all pass without an issue. It seems like all the problems we had are in the dim-and-distant past. During the day she is as confident (and annoying) as most teenagers!

The causes of Jess's sleep problem

All too often with children's difficulties, the apparent problem is only a sign of something deeper. In Jess's case, not being able to sleep was part of a broader anxiety. She felt insecure – at risk, in danger – when alone in a room at home. What did she have to fear?

Both her parents were delightful people. They had done their very best for Jess. But the fact that Jess only became jumpy if at home with her parents strongly suggests that her fears were connected with her relationship to them. She was fearful of something dreadful happening unless they – and only they – were close to her. There are three aspects of her history that may have been causing this.

During the last months of the pregnancy, her mother had been under a tremendous amount of pressure at work (she had a high-powered job in an advertising agency). Several studies that have followed children from before birth into childhood prove that this increases the risk of nerviness in offspring. A stressed pregnant mother is liable to have high levels of the hormone cortisol, the one that we naturally release into the bloodstream when feeling under threat. High levels are passed through the placenta into the foetus.

The cortisol levels continue to be elevated after the birth, making such babies jumpy. But even worse, the high levels are often still found years later, at 9 or 10. So the fact that Jess's mother was under so much pressure in the last few months of the pregnancy may have created a risk of her becoming insecure at age 8.

The second experience that may have created fears of being left by her parents was that her mother had suffered from depression during her second year. By no means does this always cause insecurity, but it increases its likelihood. Jess's mother became distressed and tearful recalling how difficult it had been. She could recall Jess placing her hands over her face and refusing to look her in the eye, perhaps because she was so upset by Marion's distress.

Finally, Jess was placed in day-care at 6 months of age. If the care is unresponsive or the carers keep changing, this can also create insecurity. In Jess's case, they had only made two visits to the nursery before she was left there, and it meant that she suddenly found herself all day long in the presence of complete strangers. Marion was unaware that this might cause problems, but she recalls that 'For the first couple of weeks, she found that difficult. I remember them telling me she had her hand over her face, would not look at them.' There is the chance that this did unsettle Jess, and it certainly upset Marion: 'That was one of those bad moments where I felt quite awful, actually. I'd get to work, and I used to phone to see how she was getting on, and they said she didn't seem to want to look at them that particular day.'

Made insecure by these experiences, Jess felt nervous when at home. Only close proximity to her parents made her feel safe.

WHERE TO GO NEXT IN THE BOOK

Other LB stories that relate to this chapter:

- ♥ **Two nights away:** Stories 1 (page 27), 2 (page 37), 6 (page 73), 11 (page 126), 17 (page 178) and 18 (page 190)

- ♥ **One night away:** Stories 3 (page 44), 5 (page 66), 8 (page 94) and 20 (page 216)

- ♥ **Awaydays:** Stories 4 (page 54), 9 (page 104) and 19 (page 213)

Love Bombing

♥ **At home:** Stories 10 (page 116), 12 (page 156), 13 (page 162), 14 (page 164), 15 (page 167) and 16 (page 168)

♥ **Spending little or no money:** Stories 8 (page 94), 9 (page 104), 10 (page 116), 12 (page 156), 13 (page 162), 14 (page 164), 15 (page 167) and 16 (page 168)

♥ **Children aged 7–9:** Stories 6 (page 73), 8 (page 94), 11 (page 126), 12 (page 156), 13 (page 162), 14 (page 164) and 20 (page 216)

♥ **Single parent:** Stories 1 (page 27), 8 (page 94), 10 (page 116) and 19 (page 213)

SIX

Hyperactivity

ADHD (Attention Deficit Hyperactivity Disorder), to give it its formal label, has become an increasingly widely used diagnosis by doctors, applied to a great many children who would previously have just been dubbed 'difficult'. One reason for this is that drug companies have persuaded doctors to prescribe drugs for children who attract this label. Whilst these drugs do reduce the symptoms in some children and provide desperate parents with some relief, there are many worries about the side-effects of taking the drugs, especially if they are taken for years on end.

In many cases, I have found it more helpful to regard very active and inattentive children as extremely anxious because they are insecure. Frequently, they act like they are permanently under threat. That makes them secrete abnormal levels of the 'fight–flight' chemical, cortisol. They are 'wired', like an adult who has just sniffed a large quantity of the drug amphetamine (which is, ironically, the key ingredient of many of the drugs given to 'cure' ADHD: weirdly and for reasons doctors cannot explain, if children are given amphetamine it actually calms them down). The reasons they are feeling so threatened are often of the kind described at the beginning of Chapters Two and Three: they feel very insecure and unloved, or they had felt this when they were babies or toddlers. They may also have witnessed considerable parental disharmony, or have been born preterm and very small, or have had mothers who were tremendously stressed during the pregnancy.

That Love Bombing can dramatically reduce the symptoms of ADHD or even cure it completely, at least sometimes, is suggested by the two stories that follow. The stories offer a plausible alternative to medicating your child . . .

STORY 8

One night away – single mother
Hyperactive and violent: Kim, aged 7

Kim, 7, has a sister, Chantal, who is two years older than she. Their mother, Polly, separated from their violent father when Kim was 3 months old.

Kim's problems

Polly recalls the first really major violent incident when Kim was 3½, shortly after moving into a new home. Her daughters were playing upstairs, and she could hear the sound of Chantal gagging, as if she was being sick. Racing up there, she found Chantal in floods of tears, Kim furiously kicking at a door. It emerged that Kim had put her hands around Chantal's neck and squeezed so hard that, as Chantal said, 'It got to the point where I couldn't breathe and that's when I was sick.'

Kim is still constantly, daily, attacking Chantal. Only yesterday Kim had been trying to stab Chantal with a pen and threatening to punch her in the face, using very extreme language. Polly wondered, 'Where does she even get that language from? I don't use it, I don't say, "I'm going to smack you in the head." I think it's disgusting, and I can't believe she says things like that.'

Kim's aggression was not only against her sister. Her attitude to Polly was a mixture of extreme hostility and desperate craving for attention. Polly recalled that 'If I was with her and I turned around to talk to someone else, she'd chew on my arm or my leg, anything she could get her teeth into, to make me pay attention to her.' Yet Kim also told Polly on a regular basis that she wanted her dead and to leave her alone, that she had had enough of her. Polly would wake to the sound of Kim snarling. She would growl, a 'grrrrrr' noise. Polly would ask, 'Why are you doing that? It's ridiculous, you're not an animal.'

In the local neighbourhood, Kim gained the nickname of 'The Terror' because she was so violent and frenetic. She was frantically active, unable to sit still at mealtimes, fidgety, incapable of attending for even a short time if asked to learn her alphabet or other basic educational tasks. Even watching a film or TV programme required too much concentration.

In the last four years, various experts have suggested that Kim suffers from ADHD and have sought to help Polly manage her behaviour. To control the biting, she was taught to praise good behaviour and deal with the bad by putting Kim on a naughty step for 3 minutes. This did not work, but, thankfully, Kim grew out of the biting by the age of 5.

Polly was sent on a parenting programme but says, 'That made no difference because she doesn't care for discipline, she's not bothered. You put your foot down and she'll increase her anger and that's when the throwing herself out of windows and clawing at her legs starts, savage scratching. I say, "Don't do that, you're going to hurt yourself", and she says, "I don't care, I hate you."' Finally, the doctor referred Kim to a child mental health centre. There, says Polly, 'She just plays – there's a girls' group, they call it the "girls of glitter group". I let her carry on because she loves it, but I don't feel this is giving her what we all need.'

By the time I spoke with Polly, she was at her wits' end. Their general practitioner was strongly advocating that Kim be prescribed Ritalin, a drug used for children with ADHD. Polly was extremely reluctant to go down that road.

The LB

As a single mother, organizing even 24 hours of time alone with Kim was not easy. Fortunately, Chantal was happy to spend a night away with Polly's parents, who live some distance away.

Having delivered her there, she and Kim returned to their home. Polly focused heavily on showing affection. She says they 'spent hours and hours just kissing and cuddling, always telling her how well she was doing, saying she was doing great. In the end she didn't want to go out and play with her friends, she wanted to stay with Mummy, and that's a first for our Kim. So I was surprised with that but it was nice.'

The feeling of closeness evolved slowly. To begin with she kept pushing Polly away. So Polly put on a DVD that Kim sometimes likes, and they cuddled up on the sofa with a quilt. Polly hugged her tight and kept playing with her hair and tickling her back. At first her response was, 'What are you doing?'

Says Polly, 'She slowly got into it, it took her a while. At first she was asking, "Why are you doing this?" when I was sitting her down, hugging her and saying "You're a beautiful little girl, you make Mummy laugh all the time, you're so funny", and just boosting her self-esteem and her ego. At first she was like "What?!" But after a while she actually really enjoyed it.'

Polly also created a game to bring them closer. She would draw a picture on a piece of paper and pin it on Kim's back, and Kim had to guess what it was. She would guess it was a house or a cat. Then Polly would write a word and ask, 'Does that say Mummy, does that say Kim?' When she got something right, Polly would be very tactile, giving kisses and hugs.

The only time they left the house was for a brief visit to the park, where Kim was 'as good as gold'.

They slept in the same bed that night, with Kim completely relaxed for the first time Polly could remember since she had been a baby. Afterwards, Polly reflected that 'I had thought I was quite tactile and very loving but obviously not as much as I could have been.'

The effect of the LB

This was one of those cases where there was an overnight transformation.

The next morning they drove to Polly's parents' house to pick up Chantal, and the family were astonished. Her parents said, 'She's completely different!' Instead of running through the door and snarling, she walked in calmly and politely and said hello. Polly was astonished.

A basic change has also occurred in how she deals with Chantal. Years of bad behaviour had led Polly to assume that all problems were Kim's fault. From after the weekend, she was at pains to avoid assuming this. She says, 'I definitely checked myself. If the girls were bickering, I wasn't going to demonize Kim straight away, I would ask them "What's happened?" and they would sit there and tell me. I never say, "Kim, I think you're to blame", which I think I probably did before, without realizing. Now, she doesn't seem to be doing anything she shouldn't be doing. She will sit down peacefully in the front room, and it is a completely different child. I was so shocked, I really was, to see the change so quickly.'

The mornings, which used to be a corpse-spattered battle-field, have become harmonious. Because Kim usually wakes earlier than Chantal, she is downstairs having breakfast with Polly. In that period before Chantal gets up, they kiss and hug, with Kim on Polly's lap. Polly plays with her hair in the way she likes. When Chantal arrives, there are no attacks on her, and Kim holds Polly's hand on the way to school, which she never would have before. She is constantly saying, 'I love you Mummy', with Polly replying, 'I love you too'. Says Polly, 'It's like the von Trapp family, just lovely. Kim's attitude to me is an awful lot more loving. She wants to sit and talk, completely new.'

Kim quite often comes into Polly's bed at night now. On one occasion she said, 'You don't like me, do you?', and Polly replied, 'Of course I do, I love you to bits.' Kim said, 'But you're not hug-ging me now', so Polly said, 'Come here', pulled her tight, and they hugged until Kim fell asleep.

There was one major altercation in the car, including attacks on Chantal and reversion to biting, but it was dealt with suc-cessfully. Says Polly, 'When we got back home we all sat round the table and discussed why we were feeling angry, why we were feeling sad and what we should be doing to get along well. We all said sorry to each other, and it was completely forgotten about after that, it was really nice. Before, you would have had tantrums from Kim several times a day, and what I've had is two in the last week.'

The relationship with Chantal is much more harmonious. Polly says, 'They still have their normal children's bickering, but it's not the fisticuffs like it was before, where Kim wants to hit and stab and bite and punch. We've not had any of that apart from the time in the car.'

Polly has had to pay attention to Chantal if Kim is around, because she does not want Chantal being left out. If Kim's had a couple of nights in her bed, she has explained to Chantal why, that they are trying to change everything, and then Chantal has had a night in her bed with cuddles as well. Because she is older, she seems able to accept the need to give Kim special attention, and she appreciates the improvement in her behaviour. Polly reports that 'If I say to her "Mummy's got to do this with Kim so we can try and stop the tantrums", she's "Ok, I understand that."'

The relationship is different as a result. As Polly says, 'Kim got up one morning, got dressed and then got a game for them to sit and play, and I was, like, "Oh my gosh!" Usually Kim's saying, "I wanna win, this is how you play this game", but this time she was playing it properly – "What colours do you want to be?" – and she was having a proper discussion with her sister. That has changed completely and it's brilliant. And to see Kim go "Chantal, give us a kiss" and swing her around, it's amazing to watch. Of course, they're not like that 24 hours a day, they've still got the sisterly bickering, but it's not physical any more.'

Chantal is not getting kicked and punched every day, so she is more inclined to talk to Kim. Now Chantal can say, 'Kim, do you want to come and play this with me?' 'Kim, shall we get that out?', and they talk to each other 'properly'. Polly says that 'Chantal is definitely more relaxed and happier. She was very quiet, and that worried me, she was very suppressed by Kim. But now they're dancing around the front room, they've got the music channel on, and she's not in fear that Kim's going to jump on her and hurt her in some way; she can actually stand there and dance with Kim, have fun, enjoy herself. So yeah, it's been fantastic for everybody.'

Above all, Kim no longer seems to assume her mother hates her, and Polly is very careful to avoid assuming that Kim is the cause of every problem. Says Polly, 'She always felt before that I was attacking her: "Mummy hates me anyway, so it doesn't matter if I do this or that, I'm going to get told off anyway!" Thinking back, that's probably how it did come across to her, because to me she always seemed to be doing something wrong. But now she gets up in the morning – "good morning" – she's happy to chat to you, so she's definitely an awful lot happier now than she was before, she's much more relaxed and she doesn't feel she needs to be in your face and hyperactive, like she was. She's quite comfortable sitting down and watching a DVD: last night she watched a whole film, and she's never done that before: she had to get up and run around. But last night she was able to just sit there, no shouting at her required, none of the "don't do that, I can't hear this". She is much more laid back and relaxed now. What I feel is that I've got my baby back again.'

At the following visit to the surgery, the doctor accepted that there is no longer a need to consider Kim as suffering from ADHD and to prescribe medication.

The causes of Kim's problems

Speaking with Polly a year later, she confirmed that the transformation in Kim had been maintained. Whereas the feeling of control is more vital in other cases, in this one it seems to have been that of feeling loved. Kim appears to have regressed to being a toddler or even a baby for periods of time during the 24 hours of LB, and this seems to have suddenly enabled her to feel loved for most of the rest of the time. When Kim felt herself slipping back into the old pattern, she was able to go to Polly for Top-Ups, most notably sleeping in her bed from time to time. At other times, she was suddenly able to tell her mother she loved her and to feel loved.

Hyperactivity

A contributory factor to the change, although not the main cause, may have been a sudden alteration in diet. From two weeks before the LB weekend, when we first discussed Kim, Polly stopped her from eating any foods with additives in them. That this was not the sole cause of her sudden change in behaviour is proven by the fact that the tantrums still occurred until the LB weekend. However, it may have created more fertile soil for the LB.

At first, Kim was angry, saying, 'I want sweets. That's not fair', but after a while she saw something on the television suggesting that sweets were harmful, and then she laughed: 'See – you live longer if you don't have sugar.' When they went into shops she would look at all the ingredients, and if she saw the word 'sugar', she would put the item back. She quickly shifted to enjoying nuts, raisins, sunflower seeds and felt happy with moving to a packed lunch instead of school lunch.

There is good evidence that diet is linked to violent behaviour in children and adults. A recent study established this by following a large, nationally representative British sample from their birth in 1970. It found that men who had daily eaten confectionery when aged 10 were significantly more likely to be violent at age 34. The researchers showed that this was more than just a coincidence.

It remained true after other key variables had been taken into account, like how the boys were cared for by their parents at age 5 (harsh physical punishment being the major cause of violence). In all, at age 34, 69% of those who were violent had been sweet-munchers when aged 10, compared with 42% of those who were non-violent.

The most likely explanation is that sweets were being used by parents in childhood as a short-term reward. This decreased the boys' ability to delay gratification, making them more impulsive and easily frustrated when thwarted, characteristics that are more common in people who use violence rather than words to express their anger.

But there may also be a direct biological effect of the sweets. Additives in them have been shown to increase the risk of acting out – of putting thoughts into action rather than reflecting on the consequences or causes of the impulse. As children, it may have made them more violent, but this has also lasted into later life. Having acquired a taste for sweets, the violent men may have gone on eating them in adulthood and still been exposed to the biological impact of additives on their behaviour.

If childhood sweet-eating does cause violence, it would fit with a number of studies in both convicted violent men and children with ADHD in which controlled diets have been shown to reduce violence.

Having said all this, it is important to reiterate that just removing the additive-containing foods was not enough: Kim's tantrums and violent behaviour only ended after the 24-hour LB. The fundamental causes of her problems lay in Polly's own history and in her relationships with men.

Polly herself had grown up with one sister. Her mother was depressed and also suffered from physical illness. As the oldest, Polly tended to get blamed by her mother when things went wrong. Just as Polly had got into the habit of always assuming that Kim was to blame for problems, so it had been between Polly and her sister: her mother had blamed her. When she saw Chantal being bullied by Kim, it made Polly extremely angry and upset, and she would come down very hard on Kim.

She recalls that 'There was always me and my sister aggravating each other, especially her telling lies about me to get me into trouble. I saw Kim and Chantal being extremely like that, actually. I couldn't tell the difference between who's telling me a lie and who's telling me the truth with them two. But I instinctively thought, "It's Kim, it's always Kim, it's got to be her somewhere that's doing the wrong." In fact, it wasn't instinctive, it was because of what had happened in my childhood. Then, to make matters worse, I would feel guilty for victimizing Kim, and that would make me even harder on her. I didn't want to get a wedge pushed between her and me, become one-sided with Chantal and not sided with Kim, which is how I had felt as a child – my Mum being with my sister and not with me. I've always said I want to do everything completely different to how I remember it. Now, at last, I can.'

An added complication was that her husband had been a violent alcoholic and a tormenting man whom Polly had finally asked to leave when Kim was 3 months old. They had met when she was 14 and had married when she was 18. Having been horribly bullied by him, she feels that witnessing Kim's violent behaviour upset her even more on behalf of the victim (Chantal), making her overreact.

A further complication was that, following the end of her marriage, she had found a new man, who had slowly become part of the family. They were going to get married. Kim became attached to him, but, to everyone's horror, at the very last minute he absconded, and the marriage was called off. Although it was no fault of Polly's, Kim blamed the end of the relationship on her mother. Indeed, this incident may have been the main cause of Kim's extremely aggressive behaviour, because it only began after the man had ditched Kim.

Doubtless all these factors played their part in upsetting Kim. The startling moral of this story is that if a mother can analyse her own behaviour and how it is affecting the way she is reacting to an extremely difficult child, and if she can then offer unconditional love for 24 hours and provide Top-Ups afterwards, there can be a total and lasting transformation in the child's behaviour.

STORY 9

One awayday
Hyperactive, insecure identical twins:
Claire and Loki, aged 4½

Paula has identical twin daughters, Claire and Loki. They were aged 4½ when she did LB with them. Paula's husband is highly supportive.

Born very prematurely and underweight, they had been in intensive care for 5 weeks and remained in hospital for a total of 10 weeks. Loki was particularly underweight, only 2 lb at birth, and it seemed unlikely she would survive. Their prematurity seems to have been the cause of great insecurity.

The twins' problems

Both girls have been very clingy to Paula and extremely anxious when separated from her, crying inconsolably. Paula says, 'They are so intense in their need for me to be there and to manage their day calmly. They do not want to be left. Even now, they have never been on a play date, and I don't want to force them.' They also cling to each other, the LB being one of just a handful of occasions in their life when they were apart for an extended period.

They have not slept well all their lives, and since starting school recently they have both suffered from nightmares.

They have great difficulty in concentrating, becoming fidgety if required to sit still for any length of time. Neither finds it easy to settle to learning to read or to practising writing. It has been suggested by various professionals that they suffer from ADHD.

They are hypersensitive, very easily distressed. They prefer watching television programmes for much younger children, because those aimed at their own age group frighten them. When upset, they rarely hit or kick but, rather, burst into tears.

Paula believes that they are not emotionally mature enough to be at school and that attendance there is greatly exacerbating their problems. Whilst Loki is coping relatively well, Claire is particularly disturbed by it. Paula reports that 'I was told when she was worst (retching on the way to school, not wanting to go to bed) that the teachers had decided to treat her differently by giving the tears no attention. She has cried about school nearly every night for the last five months, and in the morning, before leaving, she complains about stomach-aches. She also doesn't want to go to bed when she knows it's school the next morning. They both often have two or three nightmares a night. Claire will have at least one specifically about school. I know, because she will tell me in the night or talk in her sleep. The nightmares started at the beginning of school.'

Paula feels that the response of the teachers has been inappropriate. Trained in behaviour modification principles, they believe that ignoring this 'attention-seeking' will make it decrease. The approach has clearly not worked. Paula says that Claire 'cannot handle being told off. She told me that she can't breathe when it happens. She sometimes forgets to say "sorry" and she struggles because she knows that she must not cry, the teachers have forbidden it. If she is told off, she gets anxious and has to keep talking about it. She can't separate being told off from not being liked. In the middle of the night, in her dreams, she replays the words used, the face, the tone of voice and actions. I suspect the teachers think that if I treated her differently, she would behave differently. I have read enough to know I am doing okay, so I feel frustrated and patronized when they claim she is playing me up.'

Indeed, Paula is firm with her daughters, provides boundaries, and it is not likely that her current mothering strategy is the cause of the twins' anxieties. Her disciplinary approach is, 'If they are disobedient, I am very careful to avoid being harsh, I don't do the Naughty Step that often. Rather, I just say, "You need to have a sit down and think about that." I am firm but I do not get angry. If one has hurt the other, I never smack or shout, I am stern but very careful to avoid adding to the agitation and stress.' She is very aware that the girls support each other. 'If I tell one off, the other will say, "Don't be mean to my sister" and cuddle her. If one gets hurt, a scratch or something, the other will be very protective.' During their last period in hospital as newborns, they were in a cot together, and Loki stopped losing weight and stopped crying. When Claire was discharged a week earlier than Loki, she lost weight again, and Paula insisted they let her take her home.

There is good reason to suppose that the school had badly misread the situation. Claire tells her mother that 'I get tired talking to children. I need Mummy. I can't hear the teacher because I am thinking about you.' The teachers are insensitive to the fact that the twins use each other to feel secure. There are three playtimes, during which the girls are often separated. It is only when they have each other that they can cope, especially Claire. Because the teachers do not explain when one or the other of them is going off to do something, they become tremendously anxious when the other is not in view.

To begin with, at school, Claire was retching, sitting on the potty, and crying all the way there. The school admitted that she was frequently crying there and agreed that they were 'treating her differently and being a bit harder on her, to help her get over it'. Despite accepting that she was highly distressed, they also maintained that it would be 'fine'.

Hyperactivity

Paula is convinced that, owing to their immaturity, the twins are too young to be at school. She believes that the teachers and other professionals are mistaken when they try to persuade her that she is being overprotective and that this is causing their clinginess. Until they are older, she is determined to hold the twins back from schooling altogether, or at least to insist that they only go for mornings.

The LB

Given how anxious the twins are at night, Paula did not feel that it would be sensible to spend one, let alone two, nights away with one of them. Fortunately, planning a day away was feasible because both twins are now able to be with their father or grandmother without distress.

The main difficulty Paula confronted was that the twins were so unused to being apart for extended periods. The few times they have been on their own, she said, 'they turn into different children. They don't know what to do with themselves, it's quite uncomfortable.' This lack of identity, not uncommon in identical twins, has naturally affected their capacity to identify activities that they would uniquely enjoy on the LB day. When asked, 'What would you like to do, how would you like the day to play out?', they struggled. Eventually, Paula managed to extract from them names for their days. Claire's was Rainbow Glitter Day, Loki called hers Shiny Happy Day,

Loki was the least comfortable with the idea. Paula recalls that 'She said, "I've never done it before, and I'm scared."' Says Paula, 'Loki is the one that I took a long time to bond with, she was in hospital longer than Claire. She's the one I always wanted to get more of a bond with and who fought me more on having this day, worried it would exclude Claire, that she would be sad. Loki was crying on the doorstep, and I almost didn't go. I thought, "What am I doing?" Eventually, when she realized she was having a nice time, she got into it. They're never allowed to do what they want, because one always wants to do the complete opposite.'

In the event, it proved a potent experience. Reports Paula, 'It was lovely that Loki could walk into the balloon shop that she chose, choose what she wanted, stay there as long as she wished. All those little things were making her start to feel "Ooh, this is nice, what shall I decide to do next?" We went to the park and played badminton, then we sat on a rug and had a picnic and a nice chat about her time in hospital. I showed her some pictures I had picked out that I had never shown her before, ones that weren't too gruesome with too many tubes sticking out of her. She loved it, fascinated by the incubator. I had read a book called *Born Too Early: Hidden Handicaps of Premature Children* by Jonna Jensen. It is spot-on about how the girls behave, little things like being terrified of going to the doctor's or the hospital. In the pram, they hated having a see-through rain cover because it reminded them of the incubator. We talked about her fears. She was very obsessed with injections and asked, 'What does the doctor do to me?' Their hands and feet are speckled with white dots where so many lines were put into them when in hospital. I pointed that out to her, which I had never done before. I was pleased that she was fascinated rather than scared about hearing this, I kept it very light-hearted and didn't go into too much detail.'

It was a chance for Paula to help Loki understand her history. 'I did explain that I was very sad about leaving her every evening in hospital, that it had been very hard for me, but I knew they were safe. I tried to let her know it wasn't because I didn't love her that I had left her. I told her I had wanted to have them with me in my bed, to cuddle them. She found that a little unsettling, but then she asked, "Were you excited when I came home, and what did you do then, where did we sleep?", a lot of detail which it was nice to remind her of.'

The day out was a success, and it was much the same with Claire, including the explanation of what had happened when she was a newborn.

The immediate effect of the LB

Paula was amazed at how different their time was one-on-one. She felt able to connect with them in a personal way, especially with Loki.

Subsequently, she concluded that her instinct that removing them from school for at least another year was correct. Having done so, they are much less anxious and sleep much better.

Above all, the LB enabled them to become more separated and independent. They are still very close to each other, but both have gained a sense of their autonomous existence, two girls with differing wishes and intentions.

The effect of the LB one year later

Paula sent me an email reporting progress.

I obtained an independent report from a psychologist on the needs of the twins and showed it to their teachers. They were suddenly worried, interested in how they could help, and instigated regular meetings with the Head and their teachers to discuss the girls' progress. Within weeks Claire's physical anxiety had reduced. I am just sad and disappointed that she was so anxious and unhappy for six months before anyone would acknowledge anything was wrong. She still finds school and being separated from me extremely hard. They both do, but especially Claire seemed to tick every box for hyperactivity. I must do some more Love Bombing with Claire as it has helped with her separation anxiety in the past.

The Love Bombing for Loki has made a huge difference. As I said, I found it very hard to be with her on my own. I think for a long time I carried a lot of guilt for "letting go" to a degree while she was in hospital. Unlike Claire, she was incredibly small, fragile, and didn't seem to relax so well with me. She reminded me of the baby I had lost [Paula had lost a baby before the twins were born], and if I'm honest, I didn't think she was going to make it. She was more relaxed with Rob [Paula's husband], so I always spent more time with Claire. I feel strongly that she felt abandoned and, later on, could perhaps not understand the anger she often felt towards me. I don't know if I told you this, but after the Love Bombing she told me she kept having a dream where she was surrounded by 'black' people (she meant dark figures) in hospital that wanted to do injections, and she kept trying to tell them there was nothing wrong. Again, I strongly believe her subconscious has retained the awful experience she had to endure.

But the Love Bombing was sustained. It's like the missing link has been put into my relationship with Loki. It actually makes me well up to think about it. If ever I feel us drifting apart, we spend some time alone, reading and chatting. We get out her special stone. I remind her how special she is and how much I love her, and we are back on track. Since then she has also not had a repeat of her nightmare, and our relationship feels normal.

I believe that after the Love Bombing there was a change in our connection, whether it is in her brain, nervous system or the very cells that make us up, perhaps all of them. I don't know, but the way she is with me, even the way she looks at me, is different. Since the Love Bombing, she has stayed more open and affectionate with me, regularly wanting to cuddle me, saying that she loves me more than all the stars in the sky! I have always had this with Claire, but to have Loki be so loving and trusting is fantastic! The impact on my family's life is huge. I will be forever grateful. How experiences affect us physically as well as mentally fascinates me and is something that I shall study further.

In both cases, there has been a significant decrease in the amount of hyperactivity in the girls, a decrease seemingly brought about by the LB.

The causes of the twins' insecurity

There are many studies proving that severely premature and underweight children are much more likely to be anxious and to have many other related problems. Paula realizes that the trouble started before they were even born. 'They had so much against them by then. I had lost a baby only 11 months before they were born, so I was hyper-stressed during the pregnancy. My business had started to lose money. Then the twins had reflux for the first two years, which made things very difficult.'

There was the usual problem with twins of giving each individual attention. 'Whenever I picked one up, the other was crying. They were very wired, anxious little babies. I still sleep with them now, on a single bed in-between theirs. I did wonder all along if a lot of my need to pick them up and be close to them was mine, but I realize now they really do need it. The nurses, the health visitors, everyone told me the opposite: "Put them down: they'll get used to you picking them up if you keep doing it, and then you will have more of a battle on your hands because there's two." The nurses in the hospital were awful. One time, Loki was being given a blood transfusion and I picked up her up and told her, "Oh, darling, you've had a horrible time this morning", and the nurse said, "No she hasn't. She probably needs this transfusion because you are picking her up too much and making her tired!" I used to sit by the cot thinking, "I mustn't pick you up, you must rest", but it was against every instinct. I feel quite angry now that I was told to do the complete opposite of what I felt was right. I have since learnt from *BLISS* – the organization for parents of premature children – that babies which are held by their mothers in the neonatal unit actually leave earlier.'

A major problem was that Paula took much longer to bond with Loki than with Claire. She says, 'I didn't think that Loki was going to make it, she was under 2 lb. It took me about two years to properly bond with her. I had been warned that there is a tendency for mothers to relate more to the bigger, stronger child, and I was sure it wouldn't happen to me, but it did. I think a lot of women don't realize they haven't bonded with their babies, but because I had twins, I did: I could see the difference in how I felt towards each one. When Claire was near me, her smell almost set off a physical reaction in me. Holding Loki, even though I loved her, it was almost like holding an adopted child. I had no physical connection with her. I would deal with them in exactly the same way, give the same kind and amount of attention. But I felt like I didn't know Loki, which was bizarre because they look exactly the same. With her, it was a mechanical response, feeding, picking up and so on, but emotionless. With Claire it felt nice, viscerally different.' Paula believes that the LB enabled her to correct some of this deficit in her early bond with Loki.

This difference had its roots in Paula's own childhood and infancy. 'My Mum was detached, depressed, irritable, smacked us. She was either shouting at my Dad or at us. My sister was exactly the same with her children. I vowed I would never be like that.' What seems to have happened in the early years with the twins was a split in Paula's experience. She did repeat her own experience of neglect by giving it to Loki. On the other hand, the part of her that wanted to avoid doing so was expressed towards Claire.

This is a common response to having a baby. In meeting their needs, some mothers are giving them an experience of the mothering they never had. So long as it is not done intrusively or using the baby as a comforter, it is a very healthy way of expressing one's own childhood distress. The commonest difficulty for such mothers is in separating from the baby when he becomes older.

On the other hand, some mothers simply reproduce what was done to them, as Paula's sister seems to have done. Indeed, for the first two years, that is what happened with Loki.

It is possible that the teachers and other professionals misinterpreted Paula's concern for her children as over-control and anxiety at being separated from them. In fact, as the evidence clearly shows, many underweight babies turn into children who develop at a slower rate. In insisting that her twins not be required to do 'too much, too young', Paula was right and the professionals were wrong.

WHERE TO GO NEXT IN THE BOOK

Other LB stories that relate to this chapter:

- ♥ **Two nights away:** Stories 1 (page 27), 2 (page 37), 6 (page 73), 11 (page 126), 17 (page 178) and 18 (page 190)

- ♥ **One night away:** Stories 3 (page 44), 5 (page 66), 7 (page 86) and 20 (page 216)

- ♥ **Awaydays:** Stories 4 (page 54) and 19 (page 213)

Love Bombing

- ♥ **At home:** Stories 10 (page 116), 12 (page 156), 13 (page 162), 14 (page 164), 15 (page 167) and 16 (page 168)

- ♥ **Spending little or no money:** Stories 10 (page 116), 12 (page 156), 13 (page 162), 14 (page 164), 15 (page 167) and 16 (page 168)

- ♥ **Children aged 3–6:** Stories 2 (page 37), 3 (page 44), 4 (page 54), 5 (page 66), 14 (page 164), 15 (page 167) and 16 (page 168)

- ♥ **Children aged 7–9:** Stories 6 (page 73), 7 (page 86), 11 (page 126), 12 (page 156), 13 (page 162), 14 (page 164) and 20 (page 216)

- ♥ **Single parent:** Stories 1 (page 27), 10 (page 116) and 19 (page 213)

- ♥ **Children who were born preterm:** Story 11 (page 126)

SEVEN

Perfectionism

Perfectionism means feeling that your best is never good enough. It is nearly always accompanied by a highly self-critical mind-set, to the point of depression. There are often obsessive tendencies such as the compulsive repeating of behaviours or thoughts in an almost superstitious attempt to protect oneself, or sometimes getting bogged down in detail and being distracted from the main goal.

Some perfectionist children have parents, especially mothers, who are the same. They may micromanage the child, being intrusively interfering, so that the child is hardly able to blow his nose without the parent suggesting a better way of doing it. There can also be a history of the child feeling he must 'save' the parent: for example, if there has been an unhappy marriage. Many perfectionists are very anxious, nervous people, made so by insecurity dating back to the early years. Sometimes their well-meaning parents have placed a much greater emphasis on achievement than love. The latter may only be proffered if the former occurs: love conditional on performance.

Given all this, it is easy to see how a period of feeling intensely loved and of being in control could help the perfectionist child. It can also help the parent to change the pattern of care. That was certainly so in the following Love Bombing case.

STORY 10

24 hours at home – single mother
Perfectionism, mild OCD, locked down emotionally: Mark, aged 11

Mark, 11, has lived alone with his mother, Shauna, since his father left the family home when Mark was 9. Shauna works as a teacher, and she has been the main breadwinner in the family throughout his life. She worries that Mark has felt he has had to look after her, be The Parent, when she has been troubled.

Mark's problems

Following a stressful pregnancy and birth, Shauna says, 'Mark was born habituated to anxiety. He has lived in a chronic state of it ever since.'

She describes him as 'quite OCD' (Obsessive Compulsive Disorder – an uncontrollable need to perform repetitive, pointless rituals) about clothing, like worrying about the length of his shirt sleeves and the fit of his socks. He worries obsessively about what he eats, and how much.

He is also 'quite reserved'. She says that 'He's an amazing person, he's very bright, reads everything, but finds it hard to open up to other people. I would describe him as Locked Down.

He's very loved and the most loving person, but he finds it hard to express that.' His relationship with his peers has been awkward, and he is liable to be an outsider.

He is also hyper-self-critical, to the point of perfectionism. Shauna says, 'There would be a frequent "sorry" for everything he does. If he wrote stuff down wrong he would try to rub it out, frantically. Learning the guitar and trying to play something, he would stop at the first hurdle because it wasn't perfect, a strongly perfectionist streak. He was setting himself these impossibly high standards and seeing himself as a failure.'

Most dispiriting of all, he showed signs of depression. At times his mood seemed sad and disconsolate. A thick layer of self-criticism misted his capacity to enjoy himself.

Preparing for the LB

Shortage of money precluded ideas of a weekend away in a hotel or even a modest motel, so Shauna decided to do LB for 24 hours at home. She recalls that 'I devised my own version, based on the ideas you sent. At that time we were house-sitting for a friend, and I used the opportunity. I explained the concept to Mark. He read the protocol you sent and said, "That sounds great." I told him, "We are going to do exactly what you want to do, when you want to do it, in the order you want. It's entirely your choice, I'm here exactly for you." He didn't really believe me. He said, "Really? Really-really?" and I said, "Yes, it would be a minimum of 24 hours." It was hard to commit to longer at that time. This was all about five days before we did it. It was great that he had that time to anticipate it.'

He did not give it a name. She says, 'He understood it intellectually, but as a child he was thinking, "What? This can really happen to me?" He really looked forward to it.'

The LB 24 hours

The night before the LB day, he had asked, 'Is it alright to come into your bed?', and when he woke up, he said, 'Wow, is this really happening?' Shauna thinks he had a fear that something would interfere or take over, get in the way of it actually happening. She asked, 'When do you want your breakfast, what would you like?' He said, 'Do you want me to get it?' and she replied, 'No, I'm getting it for you.'

He had not made any plans. She feels that 'he wanted to just wake up and see how he felt. So it was a very relaxed, easy time. It was just hanging out, watching films, going for walks, having a bath when he wanted, eating what he chose when he wished.'

It seems that the crucial element was nothing to do with the specific activities, just that it was all about him. Shauna says that 'he was really astonished that he could make those choices, be in control, be so self-determined. It was a revelation that he was that important, was that significant to me or to the wider world, or ever could be.'

The loving part of the experience was important as well. Shauna recalls that 'I did loads of telling him I loved him, and cuddling. We spent time with legs tangled up together on the sofa watching stuff. That in itself is nothing new. The difference was the context. Perhaps sometimes I do it for myself, to feel loved, whereas this was for him. That gave it more value.'

The Top-Ups

Since the 24 hours was only a subtle shift in their normal daily life together, it was not difficult to incorporate it into their ordinary lives. Shauna reports that 'We have continued with Mark Choice Night. When we have a window, it'll be what he wants for dinner, what he wants in the evening, choice of the first bath, that sort of thing. Sometimes it's once a week; it depends, because we have busy lives. That works very well, such that, when things have been hard for me, like when my Mum died, he applies it to me. He said, "It's definitely Mum Choice Night" when I was upset about that. That indicates to me that he finds it significant and worthwhile.'

Having decided to do it in her own way, with the 24 hours as the foundation, Shauna feels it has become part of their daily relationship. She says, 'It was such a lovely experience and success for both of us that we naturally wanted to carry on. It's not weekly as a diary commitment, but it happens at least fortnightly. We just do it when it seems right.'

In between the LB Top-Ups, life is not radically different. During them she turns off her computer and puts work to one side, as well as Mark having the final say about what happens. Usually they are pretty democratic and will ask each other, 'What do you fancy doing tonight?' On his Choice Nights, having the power to decide is only a subtle shift.

The impact of the LB and Top-Ups

Speaking two years after the LB and introduction of the Top-Ups, Shauna believes that the 24-hour LB period created 'a huge sense of relief. When bad things have happened since then, Mark has had that period when good things could happen to fall back on. He said, "It's like when the Internet router goes wrong and you reboot it: start again." When things have been so negative and difficult and bleak, it seems like a spring day he can look back on, makes him feel that good things could happen again.'

The change in his various problems directly followed the LB. 'He was immediately less anxious, and as time has gone on, that trend has continued. He has become much more aware of his tendencies to be OCD and perfectionist, reducing them. Of course, over the two years, going from 11 to 13, that may be partly maturational, just part of his growing up.'

However, she believes that the LB enabled Mark to be more self-aware. 'He will say, "You know how OCD I am about my shirt" and then accommodate it, make a joke and not be so bothered. He will say, "I have found a way to make it okay."'

She says the perfectionism is also much reduced: 'He's seen it's okay to be fallible, good enough, so long as he has tried his best.' An important factor in this change may be that she has become skilled at nudging him out of this preoccupation. She says, 'I have tried to illustrate that good enough is perfect, because it's such a burden to carry that perfectionism. I make a point of talking out loud to myself in his hearing, "That will do, Shauna, it's okay, enough."'

She has been cultivating an irreverence, that things can be fun, you do not have to take everything too seriously. 'He will say, "Oh no, I haven't done my homework!" I'll say, "Oh dear, you'll be struck down, whatever will we do?" – that sort of thing.'

Occasionally, when playing a game, he gets really quite cross with himself. 'But he has begun to process that it's ok not to get it right first time, or even not at all.'

He is also much less perfectionist about his homework and results at school. She says, 'I suppose I am atypical as a university lecturer or parent in saying, "Don't push it too hard, sometimes even rubbish is good enough." I think that has taken some of the steam out of things, even if he is always going to have a strong drive to succeed.'

In an email to me two years after the LB, Mark (now aged 13) wrote of the experience as follows:

I'm sorry, but I can't for the life of me remember what happened on the Love Bombing day itself. But what I do remember is that nothing drastically different happened, just that it was the thought that something drastically different could happen, or I could just stay at home with Mum and do nothing. In short, it was just the thought that made it special.

About Mark Choice Nights, I'd say it's similar to Love Bombing, and again, nothing drastically different happens. Just that, as the name suggests, what happens and in what order is my choice (or Mum's choice, seeing as Mum Choice Nights have been brought in). In my opinion, I really like the idea, because it's similar to Love Bombing, but it can be done whenever.

I think all this has genuinely had an effect on the kind of person I am. It definitely boosted my 'happiness levels' and reminded me how to be cheerful. I don't even want to think about how I'd be now if Mum hadn't read one of your articles.

So, basically, thanks for everything.

Perhaps most significant of all was the way the LB experience changed the way that Shauna relates to Mark. She says, 'It made me realize that I have been letting him parent me – even sought that care – because I have been highly distressed and lonely at times, mainly as a result of the troubles with his father. Mark is a very, very sensitive person, tunes in to emotional frequencies. He used to say, "Are you ok, really ok?", never sure if I was answering honestly, so he must have been worried about me.'

She feels that 'The revelation was that he didn't have to carry everything. He has felt he has to carry me, which is awful. He started to feel he had to parent me. This was an opportunity to say, "You are going to be looked after – I come second." It reset the dynamic between us. It wasn't just that the 24 hours, the continued Top-Ups and how we started behaving in-between created a new pattern. It reminded me of my true role, the need for me to be the parent, not the child. I started to relate to him as being the someone to be looked after. In the morass of my difficulties, he has always from a young age been worried about me. After the LB, I could say, "I'm absolutely fine, and this is how we do Me looking after You." He doesn't have to carry my load, and I think he did feel he had to before.'

Shauna explained to Mark explicitly that she is the adult, he is the child. Recently her mother died, and he was less upset about losing her than at what it had done to Shauna, whether she was going to be able to cope. She reassured him that her distress was a normal part of grief. She spelt out that there would be times when she would be upset or crying, but that 'I am ok, you've got to let me handle it. If I need support I will ask.' She believes he knew that she loved him, but before the LB he had not realized that he had needs and could even ask to be looked after. The experience opened his eyes to her being his parent.

Her final conclusion is heart-warming. 'It's been absolutely fantastic, quite transforming. He had some counselling at school, and I think he found that quite difficult, couldn't open up. This, I would say, has had a much greater effect. That's pretty amazing, given it was only a 24-hour investment. He's a gorgeous boy – I know I'm biased! – but that's why I wanted him to feel better about life. It was a big deal for me, and it really has worked. Now he has the feeling that things can be alright – and what a difference is that!'

The causes of Mark's problems

During the pregnancy, Shauna was stressed about his father and worried about their finances. When he was first born, she remembers they just stayed in bed and cuddled: 'It was amazing.'

However, because her husband's income was unreliable, Shauna says she went back to work much earlier than she would have wanted, after 11 weeks. She felt that she 'had to do it and that was stressful'. Originally, the plan was for her husband to care for Mark, but he was unable to cope. Mark went to a minder, who, she recalls, 'was lovely. He was happy there, but it was difficult. I was the one who got him up and ready, and took him to the minder, I pretty much did everything. In essence, I was a single parent, although there was another around, sometimes.' They had a lot of house moves, and their lives were very unsettled.

Her husband has an itinerant job, and she is still in touch, but he is a difficult man to get close to. He would work away during the week and return home at weekends, but although she felt 'semi-detached' as a wife, Mark was attached to his father. They had a protracted split-up, with the final separation happening five years ago, when Mark was 8.

She believes that 'Mark thought it was his fault – he must have said it was his fault twenty times a day'. Mark received a terrible shock when he discovered that his father had another woman. She says that 'he'd always been anxious, but it got a lot worse after he accidentally found that out, a very unfortunate trauma'. His father was living separately at the time, and she and Mark had been away on a trip. They were supposed to be having dinner at his father's flat. Shauna recalls that 'When Mark walked in he saw a pair of women's shoes under the coffee table which he knew were obviously not mine, very delicate and a small size that mine aren't. He immediately twigged what they indicated and that was something very wrong. He picked them up and took them into the kitchen saying, "shoes, shoes, shoes" in a very distressed voice. To this day I think he would say that was very traumatic for him. He was much more anxious from then on.'

Shauna believes this experience exacerbated difficulties Mark already had. 'The perfectionism was there; he would always be slightly held back, reserved, not in the thick of things with his peers. He's a quiet person, felt peripheral with his peers. All of that was enhanced after he found the shoes.'

WHERE TO GO NEXT IN THE BOOK

Other LB stories that relate to this chapter:

♥ **Two nights away:** Stories 1 (page 27), 2 (page 37), 6 (page 73), 11 (page 126), 17 (page 178) and 18 (page 190)

♥ **One night away:** Stories 3 (page 44), 5 (page 66), 7 (page 86), 8 (page 94) and 20 (page 216)

♥ **Awaydays:** Stories 4 (page 54), 9 (page 104) and 19 (page 213)

♥ **At home:** Stories 12 (page 156), 13 (page 162), 14 (page 164), 15 (page 167) and 16 (page 168)

♥ **Spending little or no money:** Stories 8 (page 94), 9 (page 104), 12 (page 156), 13 (page 162), 14 (page 164), 15 (page 167) and 16 (page 168)

♥ **Children aged 10–13:** Stories 1 (page 27), 17 (page 178), 18 (page 190) and 19 (page 213)

♥ **Single parent:** Stories 1 (page 27), 8 (page 94) and 19 (page 213)

EIGHT

Autism

People who are diagnosed as autistic – to a greater or lesser degree – find it difficult or impossible to perceive the thoughts and feelings of others, often having restricted, repetitive, almost ritualistic ways of behaving. The extent of these problems varies in both their manner of expression and their severity, so people are on a spectrum, with extreme and pervasive autism at one end and mild and infrequent signs of it at the other.

For years, many parents may have been feeling that their child is odd or not quite 'all there' because he makes strange comments and shows a startling unawareness of the feelings of others. When the doctors tell them this is a recognized condition, it's a relief, as is the news that the diagnosis brings with it a great deal of practical, material support from an army of educational and clinical experts.

There has been a gradual extension of the autism concept to include increasing numbers of children on the spectrum. Doctors usually explain to the parents that the cause is wholly or largely genetic. Whilst it is possible that in extreme cases this is indeed true, in many others it may not be so simple. The possible problem with parents taking the view that genes explain autism is that they believe they can do nothing to change the situation. If it's purely genetic, then you can no more change the colour of your child's eyes than his autism.

My suspicion is that a proportion of what is currently being diagnosed as genetic is only partly so or, in some cases, is not genetic at all. The story that follows shows how important that can be, because if your child is only mildly autistic, it is possible that Love Bombing could make a big difference.

STORY 11

Five weekends of two nights away
Autistic, prone to meltdowns: Sara, aged 8

Sara, 8, has a much younger sister, Geraldine, aged 2. Her mother, Gemma, suffers from epilepsy; she is married to a very supportive husband. Gemma is a perceptive observer of human foibles and has pursued every avenue to help her daughter. In fact, this case is a landmark in the use of the LB method, in that she has now done five weekends away with her daughter. Without prompting, Gemma devised new ways and extended applications that have greatly helped her daughter and call into question much of the received wisdom regarding how best to conceive of the causes and treatment of Sara's problems. Although the first LB weekend had only limited success, 18 months later four subsequent ones have achieved remarkable improvements.

Sara's problems

Sara has recently received a diagnosis of Asperger's syndrome (a mild form of autism). Gemma describes Sara as 'incredibly bright, but she doesn't pick up other people's signals. Unless I am standing right in front of her shouting, she will not "get" what I am trying to convey, emotionally.' She also has obsessions. After leaving a swimming pool, it takes a long time for Sara to change out of her costume, shower, dress and dry her hair, because she has a lot of fixed patterns she is compelled to go through. On one occasion, Gemma asked her to be faster than usual because her husband had 'phoned and there was an emergency at home. Her younger sister wanted her mother, and her father was getting upset, but Sara could not understand why. Gemma explained that having a 2-year-old daughter crying can make parents unhappy, but Sara simply could not grasp why that might be upsetting her Dad. As Gemma put it, 'Sara exists in her own little bubble.' She dislikes groups. At a disco, she will act independently, not 'take part'. Recently, she burst into tears after school and said, 'We had to do something in a team: I can't do teams.' In the playground she will be hovering on the edge of a group, wanting to be part of it, but then barge in and take over without picking up the subtle rules of the game or of cooperative activity.

When playing alone with friends, it is the same. If things do not go according to her plan, she finds it intolerable and has a meltdown. For example, a little girl came round recently and was not doing exactly as Sara desired with a jungle toy. Sara started off by screaming at her 'You've got to do it like this!" The girl explained she wanted to do it differently from that, and Sara stormed out in floods of tears. She recently moved up to the junior school and has not found it easy, thumping her best friend in the stomach. Reports Gemma, 'Sara was sent for detention in a room on her own. When she got home I asked if the detention was upsetting, and she said, "It was brilliant, I got a room all on my own, they left me alone, I could do what I wanted." That was her idea of heaven.'

Over the past year, Sara has become aware that she is different from other children, that she does not fit in, and it has begun to upset her. She is easily overwhelmed by almost any demand and spends much of her waking life feeling stressed. Gemma regrets that she reacts 'appallingly' to this short-fused and angry daughter. 'I get upset and furious myself. We live in a chaotic family. There's a lot of love and fun, but it's a loud, shouty environment.'

Sara has never been fully toilet-trained. Her knickers are damp by the end of most days. At least once a week, she has a major accident. Gemma sees her wiggling and fidgeting, clearly in need of a visit to the toilet but refusing suggestions that she go. A few minutes later, she wets herself. Gemma says, 'She withholds and wets whether you nag her or not, I've tried everything.'

Sara resists almost all requests to do things she dislikes. She is particularly put out by more than one demand simultaneously, such as to brush her hair as well as her teeth. Says Gemma, 'That will throw her completely. If not nipped in the bud, it leads rapidly to floods of tears, lying on the floor kicking and screaming: A temper tantrum, like you see in a toddler.'

Gemma says, 'We do have Asperger's in my husband's side of the family. We have thought that what we have here may be a very low level of the illness.' The implication was that the problem might have been passed down through genes. But it is very important to bear in mind that, just because a trait runs in families, that does not prove it is genetic. It is just as possible that the trait is passed down through learning or imitation or maltreatment, although in the case of real autism that is much less common – it may well be the most heritable of disorders. Nonetheless, some kinds of what is called Asperger's (as opposed to full autism) may not be caused by genes at all.

Gemma has had trouble persuading Sara's teachers that

there is a problem. 'Because she doesn't throw chairs through windows at school and does well academically, I get a lot of "Don't worry, she's fine." They mean, "Go away, overprotective mother!"'

However, she has managed to persuade the child mental health team that Sara needs help. 'There is a huge gap between her intellect and emotion. I've said that, on the one hand, she is so intelligent that I am parenting a nigh-on teenager, but emotionally I have a 2-year-old, and there's very little between them. They said they would put her emotionally at 3–4, which was reassuring.'

At the point when she contacted me, Gemma was despairing. 'I really don't think things are right. She's not happy, and neither are we. I hate to admit it, but I have reached the stage where I brace myself when she is coming home or even into the room. I've been feeling we need a totally fresh start. Do we need to move house, school? New balls, please!'

Planning the LB

In discussing Sara before the weekend, Gemma and I considered two very different ways of regarding her problems and the potential efficacy of LB.

The first was to regard Sara as suffering from a genetically inherited brain deficit that limits her capacity to understand that other people have thoughts and feelings. Her difficulties with other children and in relating to her family would be a consequence of this disability (or difference from the norm, as some regard it). In this model – which is the one favoured by the medical establishment – whilst LB could help to reduce Sara's reactivity, by making her feel loved and in control, it could not be expected to change the fundamental cause of the problem.

On the other hand, it was possible that Sara has little or no genetic disposition to have these problems, that she is suffering from severe anxiety about relationships caused by her experience in the womb and beyond, making her too insecure to be able to cope with them. Whilst her experiences could have been the reason for parts of her brain to be underdeveloped or caused her to have patterns of brain chemicals and brainwaves different from other children, the cause would be different – not unchangeable genes – and the potential for improvement greater, given the plasticity of the brain. In this model, being given control and shown constant unconditional love might help to reset her emotional thermostat. She would be regarded as someone who regressed into a toddler when faced with stress or frustration. Whilst LB might not instantly change the degree of Sara's anger at frustration, it might help to foster a more harmonious relationship with Gemma which, over time, could produce fundamental change.

Regarding the LB, Gemma raised a simple issue at the outset, which is that Sara is made uncomfortable by displays of affection. She said, 'Sometimes Sara seems a bit surprised if I embrace her. She responds, but it seems like a learnt response. Other times, like if I ruffle her hair, she barks, "What the hell did you do that for?" If it's on her terms, it's fine; she objects when it's not expected or asked for by her.' The important thing was that Gemma did not express the love in a way that seemed intrusive.

It's not as if Sara never hugs her mother. 'Sometimes she will cling, she will go over the top, saying, "I love you I love you", and then hugging so tight that it's uncomfortable. She's almost forcing me to stop it. It's as if she is squeezing an object too hard, as though she does not realize I could feel pain.' This is reminiscent of a pattern of insecurity known as clinging-resistant attachment, in which the child will allow himself to be hugged or seek embraces, but, once in proximity, he wriggles or lies limp or is stiff as a board, simultaneously being close to and repelling the other person. Before the weekend, therefore, Gemma told Sara she would like to show a lot of love during the trip but that she understood she does not like that too much, so she would try and do it only when Sara wanted it.

Our hope was that feeling in control would enable Sara to feel more able to give and receive love. As Gemma put it, 'If you let her have control, she does feel more loved. If you stop her doing what she wants, she feels it as a personal attack.'

Another concern was how to deal with a temper tantrum. If Sara said she just wanted to be left alone, as she tends to at such times, what should Gemma do? The answer was to just leave her be.

Sara was excited by the idea of the weekend. She asked specifically for a hotel room with a bath, so they can bathe together. She also wanted access to a swimming pool, as she loves holding on to Gemma in the shallow end, having close proximity.

At first, Sara asked to be taken to Legoland. Gemma suspected that this was a way of testing out how sincere she was being in saying that Sara could choose what they did – she knows that Gemma dislikes theme parks. Once Gemma indicated that she was open to the idea, Sara said, 'Actually, I just want to spend some time with you because I don't think I know you very well.' Gemma wondered if she was putting it like that because she had heard someone on television say something similar, but it also seemed like a glimmer of hope. As Gemma pointed out, 'In order for her to test me, she must know of my existence and feelings, likewise if she changes a plan with a view to it affecting me. So maybe that was a sign that Asperger's is not her fundamental problem: she *does* know I have feelings?'

Most of what Sara planned entailed staying in their room and doing face packs or 'girly things': bathing, sitting around and washing hair, shopping and buying girly toys. They were 'together things, rather than on her own'. To promote this, Gemma purchased new pyjamas, new face packs, new shampoo, and she agreed to a plan to buy an outfit and a teddy. Gemma said beforehand, 'I am really, really looking forward to it, and then every so often I go into blind panic: "I'm going to mess it up, I'm going to mess it up."' She realized that the more that they could just enjoy the experience and take that home, the more it could become something that changed the trajectory of the relationship.

Finally, Sara found it hard to settle on a single name for the LB. She used Mummy Time, Girly Time, Us Time, Fun Time and Special Time. Of these, Girly Time turned out to be the most consistently employed beforehand.

The LB weekend

The Friday

When they first arrived at the hotel shortly after lunch, Gemma reiterated that this weekend was a chance for lots of hugs and love but stressed that this was up to Sara, it was her job to decide when and how much. Sara seemed 'quite chuffed' with that and gave her 'a sideways hug, but not full-on'.

Gemma was expecting Sara to be nervous and wanting to get everything straight in her head by looking round the hotel. However, Sara would not leave the room, even though she knew there was a swimming pool that she had said she was longing to see.

Sara was very excited about having a television in their bedroom. She spent a lot of the time watching it, immediately settling down with a hot chocolate from the minibar. She was so thrilled by this arrangement that she was watching things she had already seen. At this point she said she did not want to leave the room at all for the rest of the day.

She had filled a suitcase with the tiny toys and knick-knacks she loves, a menagerie of small objects constantly at her beck and call. Two of them had been Gemma's when she was a child, and the first thing Sara did on opening her suitcase was to say, 'These are for you.' She wanted her mother to have them. Said Gemma, 'I welled up. I don't know if this was planned or spontaneous, but it was so, so lovely for her to be considering me.'

They settled down for a manicure session while Sara watched the telly, taking up a couple of hours. Reported Gemma, 'Normally she hates having anything done to her, whether that be nails cut or hair brushed, but she was completely happy for me to file her nails down and paint them. However, when I said, "Would you like a hand massage with this cream?", although the words coming out of her mouth were "this is lovely", her hands were moving backwards all the time, and I was having to move further and further across the table towards her. That sums up a lot of her responses to things. She wants to pull away but over-rides that with her intellect.' It is also typical of the push–pull pattern of clinging-resistant insecurity.

After this, Gemma reminded Sara that she had wanted to go swimming, suspecting she was putting it off because she had some irrational fears. Eventually, Sara admitted she was worried the pool would be too deep, and also that on the way there she might end up accidentally walking into somebody's room. Having flushed this out, they turned off the telly and went to look at the pool. They talked about how she found it hard to move from one thing to another. Sometimes she finds it difficult to do something even though she wants to. Gemma realized that she may be underestimating the extent to which Sara is impeded by irrational fears that secretly beset her, rather than an inherent lack of empathy for others – she is too worried about herself to take others into account.

Having reached the pool, Sara decided to give it a go. Said Gemma, 'She really, really had a great time, hanging on to me as I walked around, happy to have that contact in a way she wouldn't usually if we weren't in the water. Her confidence grew enormously.' What was more, when the end came, it was painless. 'I was in the throes of what turned out to be bronchitis, so not keen on being in there too long, feeling ghastly. I had warned her we would have to get out because a swimming lesson was starting, and it was amazing, there was no problem. We met each other half-way. She picked a random time when we would get out, and there was no tantrum.'

Once out, when Gemma wanted to go into the steam room for a quick blast to clear her clogged chest, Sara would not allow it because she would be on her own. In the end, after a surprisingly calm negotiation without a tantrum, Sara let her go in and stood at the doorway. In doing this, there was an acknowledgement of Gemma having a need, something almost unprecedented, like the gift of the small toys when they had opened her suitcase in the room.

On returning to the room, Sara was jiggling around on the bed, obviously dying to go to the loo. Gemma just looked at her, with no gesture, and Sara said, 'Okay, I'll go.' Gemma was amazed that Sara had read her thoughts, as it proved that she is capable of positing that another person has thoughts and then correctly intuiting what those are. If she was missing the part of the brain that enables intuition, or if it was damaged, that would simply not be possible. In the same way that a computer without software such as Skype or Word cannot provide their functions, so it would have been with Sara's brain and intuition:

she must have a part of the brain that can 'do' intuition for this to have happened.

Rather, her erratic capacity for intuition is more reminiscent of a small child's: they also are inconsistent in how sensitive they can be to what others are feeling and thinking, varying according to their current emotional state and how cognitively advanced they are. Sara's incontinence is another way in which she resembles a toddler, along with the temper tantrums and the irrational fears.

After the visit to the loo, Sara said, 'I'm not going out of the room now.' Its newness was exciting, she said, and having her things with her and the familiar TV programmes made it feel 'very good'.

It was supper time. Food is a vexed issue, Sara is very particular (again, like a small child), and she was worrying that there would not be anything she wanted if they went to the restaurant. They ordered chips and ice cream from room service. She wanted Gemma to order an extra portion of chips but to say that they were for her. She was embarrassed about her eating habits, something that came up at every mealtime. This weekend was the first time Gemma had known her to be self-conscious about feeling odd or different. It showed a new awareness of how others might see her, and that she was on their 'radar' at all.

When Gemma raised this, Sara said, 'Stop talking about things that worry me: some things are private and I will never tell you.' In some ways, one could understand why Sara might have felt that Gemma was being over-inquisitive. Throughout the weekend, although very well-intentioned, Gemma found it hard to just get on with enjoying it and was periodically speaking with Sara as if this were therapy, which is very much not the idea in LB. When Sara said there were 'private things', Gemma said it panicked her, perhaps worrying that some kind of abusive activity might be being hidden: 'Huge alarm bells were ringing.' At the same time, Gemma was very aware that this was remarkably similar to what had happened with her own mother. She said that 'As a child I was always told to tell my mother everything, not hold things back. I don't want Sara to have that feeling, guilty at not telling me everything.'

Despite all this psychologizing, they had a lovely supper, then a little chat, then Sara wanted to play on Gemma's computer. She is very keen on screens of all kinds.

She was hugging Gemma a lot more than usual. When they had supper on the bed, she came and sat next to her. At bedtime, she got into her pyjamas without the normal conflict, telling Gemma she loved her. Sara initially snuggled for a few minutes before moving to her side and going to sleep. This physical intimacy increased as the weekend went on. Says Gemma, 'On the second day there more hugs, she had settled into it. She seemed much calmer. The control had given her a feeling of safety, she was less panicky. It meant she felt more able to give and receive love.'

The Saturday

After a good night's sleep, Sara got straight into watching television. Gemma had to insist they set off downstairs because it was too late for room service, and they needed some breakfast. Sara was relaxed about this, less stroppy than usual.

Once there, Sara ate what she wanted and then just wanted to leave the table (again, very like a small child). She had difficulty in understanding that it would be companionable to wait until Gemma had finished. She finds it hard to understand the social dimension of meals. To Sara, the goal of the morning was to set off to the toyshop to buy a build-a-bear toy. Delaying this pleasure did not make sense to her, just as it would not have done to a 3-year-old who was longing to get something she wanted.

Waiting at the bus stop, they played some games. Sara likes Gemma to tell her stories (as do 3-year-olds), so she did a 'bus' one and one about their time away together. At the shop, Sara was very focused on getting the build-a-bear kit, and as soon as it was settled she did not want to hang around. On the way back to the bus stop, Gemma had to buy something, and they also bought Sara a soft blanket to wrap herself in as a memento, talking about how it could be 'like a hug'. When they got back to the hotel, they put a squirt of their special perfume on it. Sara has still got it on her bed today and uses it every night. Says Gemma, 'It works really, really nicely. When things have been a bit tricky, she retreats with her blanket. It's been a good reminder.'

It had always been Sara's plan to buy the bear to look after, and, back at the hotel, she wanted to dress it. At night-time she wanted to undress it and put it to bed. She has always liked the dressing and undressing of dollies and soft toys, but not the parenting. Sara's younger sister will sit and chat to her dollies, explaining things, chastising if naughty. In contrast, Sara does the practical stuff, like feeding and dressing, but she does not speak with them or communicate as if the doll or bear is a person like her.

They went swimming, although by now Gemma was feeling very ill. Sara enjoyed practising different swimming strokes, but she was also being rude and pushing the boundaries. Gemma managed to make it playful and provided physical contact, and Sara became less defiant and offensive. However, Gemma had to cut the swimming short because she was feeling so ill. Sara allowed her a brief period in the steam room.

During the evening, Sara behaved 'a little bit like a spoilt brat'. For example, Gemma asked her to pass her the folder with the hotel information, and she refused. Gemma recalls that 'eventually she threw it at me, landing on my leg, painful. She burst out laughing. Me having needs wasn't in the equation. I explained that being rude and unkind wasn't acceptable even during LB; she could choose what to do but not like that. She apologized, but it was not because she was sorry, just a going through the motions.'

Soon afterwards they had a meltdown over the computer. Sara had gone to the build-a-bear website, but it did not work as she wanted. She was bashing the laptop quite hard in frustration. However, Gemma was surprised to be able to recover the situation. 'Initially I just said, "come here", and gave her a hug, which worked – usually it wouldn't, would be the worst thing to do. So we moved away from the computer and turned it off. I told her stories of trouble with computers, like writing essays at Uni that got wiped, how they never do what they are meant to, how annoying they are, and we had a good laugh. I suggested we have some food as a means of stepping away. What came next was fascinating.'

'Firstly, she said, "I want a cuddle", then she wrapped herself in her blanket and, using baby talk, cuddled up and was very sweet: "Me love you Mummy", "me want cuddles". That moment of temper had allowed us to shoot straight through to the heart of it all. It was quite amazing, she was able to be a toddler again. So we watched telly, ate our food and had a delightful evening.' This seems to have been a truly therapeutic period of full regression to being a toddler, but instead of temper tantrums, Sara became a small child who just wanted to love and be loved. This is not as strange as it may seem: it is a need we can still have as adults. For instance, many couples use baby language or child-like words and manners of expression in their most intimate exchanges.

The Sunday

The next day at breakfast Sara still had no concept of waiting for Gemma to finish before leaving. They watched television afterwards, and as they were going to have to leave, Gemma asked if she wanted a last hug. She refused at first, but after a little while she came over to have one on the bed. Gemma asked if she had had a nice time, and Sara said she wished there had been more children of her own age.

They checked out and went for a last swim. There she met another little girl whom she dominated somewhat less than is usually the case when Sara plays. When she met the girl, she greeted her like a long-lost friend: 'Hellooooo.' Recalls Gemma, 'For the first time I have ever seen in her life, she actually asked this girl her name, though admittedly only after about 15 minutes. She would still talk over the girl when she was trying to speak, insisting they do what she wanted when choosing games. Luckily, the girl seemed more mature and quite happy to go along with an overexcited, slightly wacky playmate. Sara didn't meet any of the resistance which is what tends to lead to stroppiness. There was the occasional wry smile from the girl indicating "this child's a bit odd". They had a lovely time.'

While this was going on, Gemma was allowed into the steam room. They waved to each other occasionally.

However, with the end in sight, Sara became increasingly troubled. She threw a full-on, screaming tantrum when Gemma washed her hair after the swim, even though the new friend was just outside the shower cubicle.

Gemma's husband was collecting them and was held up in traffic. Waiting in reception, Sara was anxious about whether the bags were safe with the porter and, in particular, if the bear was alright. She was getting quite panicky, then rude and cross and impatient. Gemma suggested they get the teddy, and she calmed down a little bit. They talked about what had been the best bits, and Sara listed them in order: the swimming, her new friend and the bear.

When her father arrived, there was huge panic about getting the bags and then an enormous tantrum getting into the car. Sara was expecting a DVD player for her to watch on the journey home, but at first it did not work. Her sister was incredibly friendly, but Sara largely ignored her. At one point she did offer the bear to her sister, but 'that was just to shut her up'. She stayed glued to the DVD all the way home.

The Top-Ups

The Top-Ups were done every day for the first few weeks afterwards, but whenever they could be fitted in rather than always in the evening. To begin with, nearly always all Sara wanted was to watch telly. Gemma would be sent out to get food and was sometimes allowed to sit next to Sara with her arm around her, but with not much interaction. A day arrived when it could not be done; Gemma asked if Sara liked the time together, being told 'It's okay', but it was clear it had none of the special charge of the LB weekend. It had become just like any other time with her mother.

The reminders of the weekend, like the blanket, could still work to recreate a better state. One time she was having a meltdown about homework, and Gemma said, 'Let's get this done and then we can have our Mummy Time', and it worked like a magic button. However, for the Top-Ups to work, Gemma suspected they would need longer periods together, away from the family. It is also possible that the lack of a regular time for them reduced their impact.

Three weeks later: the short-term effect of the LB

Whilst there had been some marked changes for the better, there was no respite from the tantrums and anger attacks.

Recalled Gemma about the days after they got home: 'The come-down was really foul. I was expecting adjustment issues, but I had flat refusal and rebellion over everything. A week ago she threw a monster tantrum, screaming, trying to kick down a glass door, which lasted from 3.45 to 7.30 p.m. I ended up putting her in the garden, it was so difficult. I am still finding it hard to get back from. I almost felt a line was crossed. This was relentless, so she is still flying off the handle.'

In other departments of her life, she had been a little less tolerant of her sister. There had been no reports of any changes of behaviour at school. She seemed to come home 'reasonably happy'.

On the positive side, Gemma said, 'She has been more loving, there has been more affection towards me. When things have gone wrong, I have been able to use the LB bond as something to refer back to. When snuggling up at the end of a difficult day, I can refer to it, and it's a bedrock for both of us that wasn't there before. It's a really golden experience that we can recall, which is invaluable. It underpins and supports us every day. She uses her blanket every night to comfort herself.'

Interestingly, there had been a dramatic improvement in her continence: much less wetting. Before the LB weekend, most days her knickers or tights would be damp, with a deluge every week or so. Since the weekend, she has only been damp once in three weeks and there has been only one deluge.

Gemma had also noticed recently she had been a bit better at cooperating with other children. She did not seem to need to dominate to the same degree.

Our conclusion at this point regarding the nature of Sara's problems was that she is severely anxious. Much more than Gemma had realized, Sara is plagued by irrational fears, particularly filled with concerns about how she will seem to others, such as regarding her eating habits. This is ironic, in that she also is frequently unaware of the feelings and thoughts of others. However, there were enough examples during the course of the weekend of Sara being empathic to Gemma for us to rule out the idea that she has an irrevocable, genetically caused brain disorder. When feeling in control and loved, she was able to show affection appropriately and sensitively to her mother, something it would be impossible to do if she lacked specific components of the brain for doing that. That does not mean her brain is like other children's: it is highly likely that some parts of it are underdeveloped and that she has some patterns of brain chemistry and brainwaves which are different.

Sara regresses to the behaviour of a toddler when faced by stresses that most girls of her age can tolerate. She becomes unable to be kept waiting, she needs what she wants immediately. If thwarted, she is unable to use words and ideas to deal with the feelings, swamped by frustration giving rise to aggression, resulting in temper tantrums. Exactly like a toddler, too, she finds it hard to cooperate with peers, tending to want to have things all her own way. This is completely normal in a 2-year-old. The average 18-month-old tries to grab a toy from another eight times an hour; a year later this will still happen three times an hour. Finally, just like a toddler, she is liable to be incontinent.

However, it was of particular interest that this latter problem, the incontinence, was almost cured by the LB. Whilst the tantrums are as bad as ever, there is also a much greater capacity to give and receive love. Her blanket provides a self-soothing device used by many toddlers and babies but not uncommonly resorted to by 8-year-olds when they are feeling lonely or sad. It proves useful to Sara as a bridge out of toddlerdom.

18 months later: the long-term effects of the first LB weekend and subsequent LB work

As mentioned at the outset, Gemma is unusually able and willing to seek solutions for Sara's troubles. When I spoke to her again 18 months after the LB weekend, with Sara now about to have her 10th birthday, she had evolved the LB method and had produced substantial changes in Sara, herself and their relationship.

Gemma described developing two levels of LB. There is the Ongoing Maintenance Dose, a few hours away from the family at least once a week, a sort of Top-Up Plus. This might entail a three-hour trip into town, a meal out together (Gemma is still very preoccupied by food) or other planned periods doing whatever Sara wants. In contrast, The Treatment level entails a whole weekend away, taken during the school holidays, money and time allowing: since the first one, they have managed no fewer than four in the last 18 months, always for two nights. The Treatment weekends were dubbed Special Time Away by Sara; the Maintenance periods are Special Time.

The weekends are always at the hotel where they went for the first LB weekend. Because of the frequency, Gemma managed to get a special deal with the hotel. They always have the same room, and they do the manicure. This activity has become firmly anchored as an emblem of the first weekend, whether at the hotel or at home, along with the blanket, teddy and new pyjamas they bought for it. At the hotel, they watch the very same television, sitting in the same places in the room. They go out to eat at the same place, where Sara chooses the same dishes. Because it's the holidays, sometimes it's even repeats of the same TV programmes that are being shown as she saw on the first weekend.

Sara adores the predictability and the feeling that she is returning to the same place and experience as the first weekend. No settling-in period is required: she knows exactly what she is going to get. She takes the blanket she obtained at the first LB with her everywhere, including for the weekends. The only innovation is that, when they go into the town, instead of shops they now always go to the local zoo, visiting specific animals and sections. They buy a soft toy there as the memento for each weekend.

Gemma describes the weekends as 'a very, very powerful tool'. During the period between them, Sara's behaviour tends to get a little worse, until Gemma spots it and they start planning the next one. Immediately, Sara picks up, and they are set on a better trajectory. They still go through the same process of asking, 'What do you want to do?' even though this is already decided, invariant. Despite the predictability of the plans, thinking herself forward into it, picturing it, seems to almost trigger the experience of it happening. Even if they have to tweak dates and alter plans, Sara can cope with that, knowing it is coming. When getting close to meltdowns or becoming tense in the period between LB weekends, just being reminded that there are good times, specifics of time at the weekends, will calm her. The space in the few weeks either side of the weekends has become a haven, along with the weekends themselves. Interestingly, the adjustment back to normal family life on returning – like the process of settling in when arriving – has become much easier; it is all part of a general trend for Sara to cope better with transitions.

One of the bonuses of the weekends is that they have instituted Special Time With Daddy for Sara's younger sister. The bond between those two is vastly stronger, an accidental by-product of the plan.

The two-level Maintenance and Treatment LBs seem to have produced lasting change in Sara. The most startling is that there has been a steady and significant decrease in the 'meltdown' toddler tantrum-like anger attacks. Whereas these were unaffected by the initial LB weekend, the two-level programme is gradually diminishing them. Gemma reports that 'after the first LB weekend, no day passed without a major altercation, and full nuclear meltdowns happened at least four times a week. Today, there are a maximum of two meltdowns a week, with some kind of minor "set-to" still occurring on most days. The severity of the meltdowns has decreased. The "screaming abdabs on the floor" kind are down to fortnightly occurrences.'

That the meltdowns do still occur twice weekly shows that there is still a considerable problem, but from Gemma's point of view it is a huge step in the right direction because she was beginning to feel desperate and tyrannized until the change. She says, 'We do still have meltdowns, but we have come a very long way from where we were after the first LB weekend. I can directly relate the number and severity of the meltdowns to how long it is since we last had an LB weekend. I regard that as hard evidence that the LB does have a significant and enduring effect, which wears off unless repeated.'

If Sara's brain chemicals and brainwaves had been measured from before the LB ever began, it is highly probable that considerable changes would be found – for example, in her cortisol levels. That the meltdowns have gradually become fewer and less extreme, a cumulative change, will almost certainly be reflected in Sara's brain. It is even possible that some parts of her brain that were undeveloped will have increased in size. This could be expressed in her greater stability and reduced emotional reactivity, such as in dealing with transitions. For example, the family moved house, and Sara moved schools as well. She was not someone who likes change, even small transitions, like from watching television to going to bed. Gemma observes that 'Moving both house and school would have completely thrown her in the past. We were expecting Armageddon, horrific scenes, but they never happened. She struggled, yes, but it was manageable by her. These moves have gone well, really well.'

The dramatic improvement in Sara's continence that followed the first LB weekend has been sustained. Over the 18 months there has been a steady improvement. Whereas she used to be wet all day for much of the day, now this is only true once a week at most.

Gemma partly attributes the greater continence to increased consciousness of what other people think. Before Sara started at her new school, 'She couldn't care less if people knew she had the problem. Now she does.' The LB has promoted a greater awareness of others. Gemma says, 'Now, she sometimes grasps that someone else's experience might be different from hers. She can see that clearest if she is discussing other people's social predicaments. For example, if her sister tells a story about her school friends, Sara can offer reasonable ideas about what their motives might be, like that X is being nice about Y because she is Z's best friend. She would find that harder for herself, although she's better at it. But she still will tell stories without realizing what her audience know, such as mentioning people who they could not possibly have heard of, oblivious to the confusion that might cause.'

The degree of unawareness is not random, however. Gemma believes it relates to Sara's emotional state. 'The LB has enabled her to have much more self-awareness, possibly because she is less anxious. So if we are going to have time together, she will say, "I need you to tell me that that is what is happening so I can remember it" – she realizes she has a deficit in awareness and then is able to tell me. The instruction in the protocol you give to parents preparing for LB to strongly headline to the child that something special is going to happen and that it is going occur at a particular time is especially helpful to Sara.'

There is still a habitual unawareness of others in Sara. Gemma says, 'She will chat freely with someone we meet in the street, and afterwards I will ask, "Who was that?", and she'll say, "I don't know." She works differently. She has had a successful interaction and got something out of it. But she does still very much live in a bubble.'

It seems, nonetheless, to be an increasingly permeable bubble. As Gemma reports: 'She does have a much greater awareness of others' judgements. She said to me that the children at her school don't know who she really is, which amazed me: that she could appreciate we show different sides of ourselves to different people. She realized that if she showed some sides of herself, they would not like her. That showed much greater awareness than I have given her credit for. But then she cannot be completely oblivious, like someone with severe autism, or she could never have managed to start relatively unproblematically at a new school without the other children being warned that she has a problem.'

There have been marked changes in Sara's relationship with Gemma. 'The whole LB experience has noticeably improved the way she relates to me as well as others, to such an extent that I have strongly recommended it to parents with all manner of problems. I think she has finally got the idea that, beneath it all, we love her, and that makes her more grounded. When it goes pear-shaped, she gets it back quicker, and it's not the end of the world, she is not nearly so lost. I notice that aspect becomes more consolidated after every time we go away for a full Special Time

Away weekend. When these foundations start to tremble, that's an indication we need to go away again.'

The LB programme has also required Gemma to behave differently. 'I know I have to control my tendency to try and cope with the situation by analysing it. I am better as the result of the LB at just showing my emotion to her, being natural. I find she baffles me, and it's easier to deal with her as an "interesting anomaly", remove myself from the situation. I am better at being able to enjoy her, which is not easy. I do struggle to enjoy her, LB forces me to try. I have found it personally very beneficial, and it enables both of us to get closer to the other. I think it's a great way of relating to your child: we use it with her sister, who has a very good relationship with my husband now. I would like Sara to do a weekend with him.'

The causes of Sara's problems

Gemma suffers from epileptic fits, and her health is fragile. At its simplest, Sara witnessed her mother experience epileptic fits many times when she was a baby and toddler, a frightening trauma, and she will also have been neglected during those times.

There is good reason to suppose that Sara's problems originated very early in her life, starting from before her birth. Gemma was extremely nauseous almost from the beginning of the pregnancy, right through to the end. This meant she was very stressed, making it likely that she had high levels of cortisol, which will have passed to Sara as a foetus, affecting the sort of baby she was after birth.

She had not been with her partner for long before Sara was conceived by accident. They had recently begun cohabiting in a new city and were not expecting to have children before they got married. Gemma recalls that 'I was scared out of my brain, it all happened very fast. I started fitting during a visit to the hospital when they were doing a scan of the baby. Sara was born by emergency caesarean after I had come round from a fit, and she was in her Daddy's arms 20 minutes later. I was out of it, on Diazepam [a tranquillizer], put in a side room rather than the maternity ward.' Unfortunately, this proved to be a disastrous beginning. 'They forgot to give me a bell, and I spent the first night with Sara in the cot beside me, unable to reach her, with no pain relief. When the cleaner came in, she asked why I hadn't washed, and I said, "Would you mind passing me my baby because I haven't seen her?" When a nurse finally came in, I asked for some advice on feeding and she just walked out, saying, "I don't know why you can't feed your own baby." It was not the greatest of starts.'

It took some time before the breast milk came, so Sara was bottle-fed by a variety of people. Gemma finally breastfed for four months. She was on antidepressants and anti-epileptic drugs for all of this time, which may have affected Sara. Back home, Sara slept in a crib next to the bed and was a terrible sleeper (possibly because of being born with high cortisol levels). Recalls Gemma, 'We tried all that controlled crying rubbish, which didn't work. I was given four copies of Gina Ford, but eventually threw them away. I was persuaded to wean her at age 5 months, before she was ready, she screamed the house down when given yoghurt. It was worst in the early evening. The Infacol [treatment for colic] had to be forced down her throat.'

During Sara's early years, Gemma had severe epileptic seizures and would have to be hospitalized for two-week stretches. This happened about every three months. On many occasions Sara witnessed these, and, as already noted, this was almost certainly a very considerable trauma for her, as well as resulting in her feeling emotionally deprived and insecure. The trauma could have led to her becoming dissociated – a remote, removed state of mind that can seem very similar to Asperger's – or, indeed, a proportion of what is called Asperger's may really be a form of disorder caused by trauma.

Gemma brought considerable adversities from her own past life to motherhood. She had been a very premature baby. As a teenager, there was self-harming and suicide attempts. She was taking antidepressants from age 21 and believes she had suffered depression from well before then. Her life had lurched from emotional trauma to trauma, her parents having split up when she was 11. She believes that 'My parents went wrong from when my sister was born, when I was 3. When my Dad left, I remember aged 11 thinking, "I don't get on with either of these people, but I have got to make it work with my Mum." I didn't hate them, but we were not close. Having been unable to cope with me as a baby, my Mum worked incredibly hard to build up a strong tie with me, probably too strong – she was relying on me too much. I was the oldest. I was very controlled by her. I still find it difficult to say that: if she realized I thought it, she would be very upset.'

Gemma has to fight not to be like her mother. 'She was a strong personality, we were a bunch of Amazonian women. As a result, I think I try too hard to control – several people have told me that. So when Sara came along, it was a nightmare to have a baby I could not control, I am a perfectionist. Even so, although I was expecting having a baby to be horrific, it was lovely in the early years. I enjoy it far less now because everything is such an enormous battle.' This may be because she has found it hard to let Sara be a separate person as she developed.

Just as Gemma had a deprived, lonely early infancy, Sara must have had periods when her mother was too depressed or ill to tune in to her. Toddlers and small children need responsive carers who can also respect their emerging independence. Just as Gemma's mother could not tolerate her emerging separateness when she became a toddler, so it may have been with Sara. The most likely explanation for Sara's tendency to regress to the toddler stage is that she is trying to re-experience that period but, this time, be allowed to make the developmental shifts that she missed out on first time because Gemma was too controlling (and perhaps also because of the trauma of witnessing the epileptic fits). The LB seems to have allowed some of this to have happened. That she is nearly cured of the incontinence is one sign: being allowed to regress to a toddler and to feel safe, in control and loved may explain why she very rarely wets herself now. Perhaps she no longer needs to use this as a way of feeling in control.

It is possible that Sara's symptoms of Asperger's are a manifestation of the unease she feels in the company of others, arising from massive irrational fears she has about them. Her toddler tendency also makes it hard for her to tolerate the delay in gratification that normal exchanges with others require. The idea that she has a genetically based, and therefore unchangeable, lack of a capacity to identify with the feelings of others is probably not helpful, as well as being either totally or largely incorrect. Nor is it likely that she is incapable of being mindful of the thoughts of others. The occasion on which she intuited that her mother was thinking she needed to visit the toilet seems to disprove this, emphatically. Much more probable is that she is so swamped by her own emotions and fears that for much of the time she is simply unaware of what others are thinking or feeling. When soothed by love and being ceded control during the LB, she becomes markedly more able to empathize with her mother.

However, none of this is to deny that Sara is different from other children and that being given a label could be helpful. Sara's paediatrician has just provided a formal diagnosis of Asperger's syndrome. Gemma has pursued this relentlessly, not because she believes the 'unchangeable genetic destiny' narrative by which the doctors explain it to her, but because it will have the consequence that future schools will take the problem more seriously and, above all, that Sara will get all sorts of extra resources devoted to her. If her classmates have the label explained to them, they are more likely to cut her some slack.

Nonetheless, without this label, she has made one good friend at her new school, albeit a bit of an oddball. When things go wrong between them, Sara struggles to understand. Gemma says that 'Usually it's something unbelievably obvious, and yet Sara has no idea why that would have been distressing. It's at times like that I think there is something very peculiar about her mind, something missing. Yet at times she can read me. It's confusing. It does feel like there are gaps; sometimes we bridge them, at others it doesn't seem solid. She can have intuition, but the massive anxiety shuts it down.'

Gemma gave an illustration of the anxiety. 'She was doing a maths practice paper for an exam. She is good at maths but was tired. She looked at the first question and went white as a sheet, then puce, a rapid shift that happens often in her [interestingly, these are signs of extreme activity in the anxiety system of the brain, triggered by cortisol]. She burst into tears, in a total panic – "I can't do it, I'm rubbish at maths" – faced with calculations that she can actually easily do. She is incredibly averse to any feeling of challenge, new tastes, anything marginally risky, any emotional discomfort. She closes herself down and becomes blind to her surroundings out of anxiety.'

It seems highly likely that Sara's lack of awareness of others is a product of the care she received in her early life and is only one of a raft of problems that resulted from it. Numerous studies suggest that such care produces lasting effects on the brain. By contrast, the evidence that differences in genes are responsible for this suggests they account for only 5–10% of the problem, at most.

Gemma's unique use of the LB method is a landmark in its development. Through repeated weekends and extending the Top-Ups, she seems to be gradually reducing all of Sara's symptoms, very likely altering her brain in the process. If the programme is sustained for several more years, it is possible that she will wholly cure her daughter and bring her into the normal range of behaviour of other children. If so, she will have invented a new way of helping some children who have symptoms of Asperger's syndrome.

WHERE TO GO NEXT IN THE BOOK

Other LB stories that relate to this chapter:

- ♥ **Two nights away:** Stories 1 (page 27), 2 (page 37), 6 (page 73), 17 (page 178) and 18 (page 190)

- ♥ **One night away:** Stories 3 (page 44), 5 (page 66), 7 (page 86), 8 (page 94) and 20 (page 216)

- ♥ **Awaydays:** Stories 4 (page 54), 9 (page 104) and 19 (page 213)

- ♥ **At home:** Stories 10 (page 116), 12 (page 156), 13 (page 162), 14 (page 164), 15 (page 167) and 16 (page 168)

- ♥ **Spending little or no money:** Stories 8 (page 94), 9 (page 104), 10 (page 116), 12 (page 156), 13 (page 162), 14 (page 164), 15 (page 167) and 16 (page 168)

♥ **Children who were born preterm:** Story 9 (page 104)

♥ **Children aged 7–9:** Stories 6 (page 73), 7 (page 86), 8 (page 94), 12 (page 156), 13 (page 162), 14 (page 164) and 20 (page 216)

♥ **Single parent:** Stories 1 (page 27), 8 (page 94), 10 (page 116) and 19 (page 213)

NINE

Love Bombing
in shorter bursts

Love Bombing is a recent invention. A great deal of research needs to be done to identify what sorts of problems it works with best and which variants of it are most effective for which problems. I suspect that the studies will ultimately prove that the more severe the cause and nature of the problem, the more intensive the LB needs to be. As Chapter Eight shows, it took repeated weekends away and extended Top-Ups to help Sara, a girl with autistic traits, to improve.

One of the fascinating and pleasing responses I encountered from parents when I sent them the LB protocol was the imagination they used in adapting it. In the first place, some could not afford a day or days away. In the second, going away was impractical for some, as they also had a baby. Thirdly, some felt that although the approach would be helpful, they wanted to adapt it to fit their particular child and also to their own personality and preferences.

In this chapter I describe five highly creative uses of the basic ideas, adapted to fit the parents' practical circumstances and ideas about parenting.

STORY 12
Morning half-hours
Defiance: Dawn, aged 9

The only daughter of two older parents, Dawn is a 9-year-old whom her mother, Sheila, had diagnosed as having Oppositional Defiance Disorder.

Dawn's problems

Almost every interaction with Dawn had become a battle, with Sheila telling Dawn to do something and then nagging, nattering, being critical and bickering. Before long there would come a hideous, volcanic meltdown, Dawn reduced to a screaming banshee. Sheila would sometimes be shouting and out of control too. She recalls that 'I realized I had gone beyond the pale one evening when I found myself with my knee on her back on the kitchen floor. I thought, "I have to get out of here, this is not how things should be happening."'

Sheila's response to the idea of LB

Having read the protocol of what to do that I send out to parents, Sheila found it helped her to shape a unique approach of her own. She says: 'The 48 hours away didn't appeal because I spent an enormous amount of time with her anyway. What I wanted was to alter the way I spend that time. Because I had left my job, she had got me but in another sense she had not got me, I was there but not there. I didn't feel a 48-hour love-fest was what was needed so much as changing what happened when in our house. We had moved, and we were all struggling to adapt. I wanted to make this the place where we could be in love with each other.'

The idea of LB prompted a rethink of how she was caring for Dawn. 'Reading the protocol and assimilating your approach with the rest of the research I had been doing was incredibly helpful. I had done an awful lot of reading, half of which tells you to take control, the other half to let go, but the idea of saturating her with love made perfect sense to me. LB was part of a process of respecting her independence: just simple things like asking, "What would you like to do this afternoon?" She might say, "I want you to be around, but I want to be in my bedroom."'

Sheila looked upon LB as an approach rather than a method. 'It forced me to think of ways I could show her how I loved her – sometimes telling is not enough. And also, how I could do practical things to demonstrate that I enjoyed being her mother.'

In practical terms, Sheila instituted two aspects of the LB method.

The half-hour morning LB

Mornings were often trigger points for Dawn. It could be any type of time limit or deadline, like having to get somewhere, but getting ready in the mornings was worst. Sheila and her husband Bill looked at ways they could give Dawn more time. They decided that if she chose to have a meltdown, they needed to give her the time to have one, get over it and still get out on time.

To this end, Sheila started getting up half an hour earlier every morning (except at weekends). She says, 'I made everyone a lovely breakfast (pancakes, bacon, porridge, muffins, etc.,

etc.) and would take up a freshly squeezed orange juice for her and a cup of tea for my husband. I wake her if she is not awake. But my husband stays in bed, as she normally loves to wake up and go in to spend half an hour of Daddy Time before I come up. By my getting up before her to make breakfast, she now has options. She can come down and hang out with me, or she can lounge around in bed with her father. When I come up, they are having a laugh, and it changes the whole temperature of the morning.'

This has made the transition to getting up and setting off for school much easier. 'The three of us have a dressing-up race before zooming downstairs. Then it's on with the morning. We still manage to let the hens out and feed them, eat breakfast and do violin practice and catch the school bus on time. It has been a huge success.' Effectively, Sheila managed to ensure her daughter had a brief LB session with her Dad. Given how fraught things were between her and Dawn, that proved a smart strategy.

The other practical step was a shift towards positive present-giving as a way of making Dawn feel loved by her. 'I have a stockpile of small gifts and items. I always try and find things to reward her for. If she has thrown a strop but managed to get over it quickly, I either simply acknowledge in words that I have noticed how hard she has been trying, or I reward her with a small gift (these have included knickers or socks!). This too has been successful, and I am relying on words more and gifts less now. I truly feel she thinks I am making an effort to understand her rather than beat her into my way of thinking. And I feel clearer about rewarding effort and good behaviour rather than trying to use bribery.'

As part of this policy, Sheila has tried to change the whole basis of the time they spend together. 'Instead of doing 8,000 other things at the same time, I say, "Why don't we settle down for half an hour and do something together?" The first time I suggested we play a computer game, she was "Whoa, you playing a computer game, Mummy!? Amazing!" I was giving her control, and I was doing things her way.'

Sheila noticed that she had slipped into a somewhat hyper-critical attitude to Dawn. 'When doing her homework, instead of pulling her up on a missing full stop or misspelt word, which is what I used to do, I will say something positive, like "I love the way you used adjectives in that sentence."'

The effect of the new regime

There has been a rapid reduction in the number of meltdowns, their intensity and the quickness with which Dawn recovers. Dawn is much more self-aware. Reports Sheila, 'We've noticed she's really trying hard since we introduced the changes; even if she's having meltdowns, she's quicker to come out of it. And when she's settled down, you can see on her face that she understands the problem and that she is really trying to control herself, realizes she is being destructive.'

Sheila puts a good deal of the change down to the morning LB time. 'One of the great things that has happened as a result of our morning routine and Bill spending more positive time with her is to bring her destructive oppositional behaviour much more out in the open for all of us. It used to be something that was buried at home, something that didn't happen, she would pretend it didn't exist. It was a secret, "Don't tell anyone." Now, when it does happen, because she feels safer with us and that we are trying to understand, putting ourselves out in a way that she can see is the case, rather than trick her or catch her out, she has become more open.'

Sheila gave an example. 'Yesterday evening, Bill was able to say to her, "Darling, I just want to say I noticed that when you lost your rag downstairs you pulled back quickly, got your temper under control." She beamed and joked about it, where before, if we even alluded to her temper, she would go into an almighty rage. We have learnt to go the place where she is at, rather than drag her to ours: it's incredibly rewarding. We are getting to know the child that she is rather than the one we would like her to be in theory.'

Sheila has realized that they had been expecting Dawn to fit in with them too much. 'The giving up of control is the revelation. We don't need to assert our will over her will in such an overt way. I know that that approach screams out against all received wisdom. We felt we had to be confrontational, and letting go of that has made a big difference for her. Whereas before we would take it for granted that she should behave in a manner which is good, you forget what a huge effort it can be for a child to control themselves. If I recognize now to her that I can see how hard she is trying, it means so much to her. So it's been a big change that we have been trying to understand and then making a point of showing that we are trying, so she can see we are. It's been humbling to realize how wrong we have been getting it, lacking in empathy. We lost sight of the fact that she is a delightful person. Her way of dealing with stress became anger. We have now accepted that this is how things are for her, seeking to accommodate that rather than confront it. And in fact, the more we do accommodate, the less she finds it necessary to do it. If we don't confront her head-on, she will then be able to come and say "sorry", truly contrite about how she has behaved. She is free to realize how hurtful some of the things she has said can be. She is getting some feeling of being an independent entity.'

This seems to have been the key to what Sheila took away from the LB approach, adapting it skilfully to her family. 'We were being too rigid about the rights and wrongs, and the demands for her to say sorry. It was restrictive and choking her ability to feel responsible for her actions. We had a tendency to just get on with stuff, and the child just has to come along with what we are doing. That's why it's so nice for her to have choices, rather than just us asserting our will which we fell into the habit of doing. LB helped us break that habit.'

18 months later

Sheila sent me an update, Dawn now being 10½:

> The template I came up with worked for a long time and is still ongoing, in a slightly refined way. Dawn tends to sleep longer in the mornings and often needs waking on school mornings now, which means that she does not necessarily get into bed with her Dad and have that time – we have tried to build other times in with him. However, keeping the focus on her and her needs in the morning seems to work best. She has had a lot of trouble with friendships at school lately, which has had an impact at home. It's often on a Sunday that she has low days (which usually involve being extremely rude and/or abusive to my husband or me). I guess this is linked to going to school on a Monday, but she doesn't articulate what is driving her rages. So last Sunday I let her choose exactly what we would do all day. In fact, she was slightly at a loss, but we had a quiet day and she actually enjoyed it and did not hurl abuse at me once, which was a relief to both of us (my husband was away). I still try to reward good behaviour and find things to treat – but am doing this more verbally than with gifts now.'

Sheila concluded that 'It is definitely a work in progress but one that we are all generally coping better with.'

STORY 13

An hour or two of LB, several times a week
Temper tantrums: Mick, aged 8

Sharon sent me an enthusiastic email after she had adapted the LB technique to her circumstances and tried it on her son Mick, aged 8: 'Love Bombing works! It's all about time with your child, isn't it?'

Mick is the youngest of four children, ranging in age from 8 to 15. One of them has severe autism, which has inevitably had a big effect on the family.

Sharon described Mick as 'a vociferous, wilful child, he gets very angry very quickly. I have been alarmed at the degree of rage at such a young age. We've almost allowed him it because he's got to have that safety valve. We don't admonish or scold him because he always comes round: it might take an hour or two, but he always does. He will come back and say, "Sorry Mum." I always try to give him a back door to come back through, although, of course, I do sometimes get cross. It's hard not to become a child yourself, but getting punitive is never helpful.'

Sharon believes that the reason Mick gets frustrated is lack of time devoted to him: 'He doesn't have the time with Mum or Dad lavished on him that went on the first and second. I feel a bit of guilt about that. As the youngest in a family of four he has decisions thrust upon him. We had forgotten to do the basics with him, tended to do things as a family, all together, not enough individual attention. I think I had an idealized view that they would all look out for each other. There is always competition for parental attention, however much money you have, in a family of four. Add to that our autistic son, whom we insist on including in everything, and it gets harder. Maybe we have needed Mick to be more grown-up than he is, we are trying to put an old head on young shoulders.'

What Sharon did

Given their lack of time and money, Sharon could not conceive of a way that she would be able to manage a night of LB. Instead, she says, 'What I did was break it down into small chunks. It's not about money, which is tight anyway. It's just about playing with a ball in the park and giving him choice.' Instead of extended time away, she and her very helpful partner did their best to give Mick brief bursts of love and control a couple of times at the weekend, and three or four times during the week.

His father took him to a football match, just the two of them, which Mick adored. It is something they have done several times now. His father also made a point of staying and watching Mick when he played for his local team, rather than what he used to do, which was to drop Mick off and do some shopping chores before picking him up at the end.

Sharon took him regularly to the park: 'It was enough that it was just him, no siblings, one-to-one time.' On another occasion, they went together to get a set of playing cards and found time to play with him. In the evenings they have been stricter with themselves in ensuring that he gets 10 minutes a night, without fail, of being read to or just hearing about his day.

Overall, she feels that 'The key thing is to give him a feeling of control. We have to limit the choices available, but within those options it's up to him. So I might say, "Do you want to do some cooking: what would you like to make?"'

The effect of Sharon's LB

Reporting two months later, Sharon said, 'It really has improved his self-esteem and reduced his frustration. He has matured quite a bit, moderating his behaviour. He will say, "I'm getting really cross now", articulating it, better able to regulate it.'

She suspects that an important part of its effect is that Mick is much more bonded with his father.

Reporting again one year later, this had been consolidated, mainly through the soccer. Sharon wrote to me that 'Things have chilled out with Mick considerably. He has very much got into football, and lots of energy is channelled that way. Although not really the full-on Love Bombing that you had advocated, Mick now has quite a lot of football time with just his Dad, training together, etc. I think he enjoys this one-to-one. I remember something you said which I've thought lots about since: that making siblings all do stuff together was overrated. I can see that now, although I so desperately want them to be close now and in the future, but it's also v. important that they have room to be themselves, with their own interests and space, etc. They always had that, but now I don't get twitchy if I think they have not spent much time together at the weekend, etc. Bit of a mother hen, I can see myself! Maybe Mick got lost in that.'

STORY 14

Two hours, fortnightly
Sibling rivalry: Seamus, aged 3
Estrangement from mother: Paddy, aged 7

Deirdre has three children: a 3-month-old daughter, and two sons: Paddy, aged 7, and Seamus, aged 3. She has done brief bursts of low-key LB with both her sons, impressed by how much improvement even this small amount provides.

Seamus, and what Deirdre did

Seamus finds it hard being supplanted by his younger sister. He was very much the 'Mummy's boy', then his sister came along. Having been 'the sunniest boy in the world' he became 'a little bit prone to being upset about small things and to being difficult'. She says that 'He is completely obsessed with the baby, yet he is rough with her. His first question when he gets up is, "Where's the baby?", it's the same when he gets back from school. But then he puts on this really annoying special baby voice when he is around her. His roughness with her means I am constantly having to say, "Be careful with her head", "Watch out not to step on her leg", and so on.'

Deirdre has made time to take Seamus away for brief periods alone together. She has not built this up in advance as a full LB. She just concentrates on giving him a nice time. For example, she says, 'Two weeks ago I took Seamus out for an afternoon. We went to a hotel for tea, with lots of his books. During the drive we could chat properly because there was no one else in the car. We ate sandwiches and cakes, read the books. I told him a superhero story. It was only about an hour and half, low-key, nothing demanding, it was very relaxed and was time away from me saying "don't".'

She was surprised how much effect just doing this had. 'During that time he reverted to being more like he used to. Since the baby, he seemed to have transferred his allegiance to my husband, but for a couple of days after our tea, he was much friendlier to me and paid me more attention. He was more relaxed and keen to do things with me. I would say he is still slightly better than he was two weeks ago. In return for just a two-hour burst of attention, I thought that was quite an impressive dividend!'

Paddy and what Deirdre did with him

Deirdre says that 'I've always had a more difficult relationship with Paddy. He's a much more demanding child, was a distressed baby. He isn't upset about his sister and seems in good form, though I have done a few afternoons with him. I think he needs the full LB Monty when a chance arises. He is much closer to his father than to me, and we need to change the pattern.'

Interestingly, before she read anything about LB, Deirdre had already been thinking along those lines. Before the birth of her daughter, she had twice taken Paddy away for weekends, staying at her mother's house. She recalls, 'Just doing that had a remarkably good effect, without the information about LB. It made a big, big difference, even without the Top-Ups, and I can see how they would prolong the good effects. After a few days or a week, things return to their normal state, which is by no means catastrophic but quite strife-ridden.'

As with Seamus, she takes Paddy off for a brief time together every few weeks. For example, she took him for an afternoon to visit a bookshop to choose a couple of books. She got him a hot chocolate, and he read them for a little. Then they talked happily about anything he wanted. The drive there and back, on their own, made a pleasant change.

Summarizing her thinking, Deirdre concluded: 'Given that an afternoon reaps good results, it makes me think 24 hours will be worth doing as soon as a chance arises with Seamus. I think it might need the 48 hours with Paddy, because things have always been more vexed with him. I would be very keen on trying both of those, in due course. It won't be for another year, because I will still be breastfeeding probably a bit until then.'

She finds the idea of LB very encouraging. 'The great fear is that you have done the damage and there's no way to repair it. I am convinced nothing is necessarily permanent. You end up saying "don't", "stop" all the time. LB offers a way to change the pattern from just crowd control. If you are not careful, you turn into a parental bureaucracy.'

STORY 15

LB as part of everyday life
Neediness and truculence: Greta, aged 3

Marcia and her partner George share the care of their children, both working half the week. They have a 3½-year-old daughter, Greta, and a son who is nearly 2.

Because of the small age gap, Marcia was concerned that Greta was not getting the one-to-one time she feels she needs.

The LB

Marcia reports that 'We already did scaled-down "Love Bomb" sessions with our daughter. It doesn't happen on a daily basis but usually three or four times a week. When her younger brother sleeps in the afternoon, whoever is looking after the children usually spends time "Love Bombing" with Greta. The time can be anything from half an hour to two or three hours, depending on what else is going on, but the activities are directed by her. Very often it is as simple as reading books and cuddling on the sofa; sometimes it's crafts or games, but essentially, the time we spend doing this is very focused on her and what she wants.'

The effect of the LB sessions

Says Marcia, 'I am convinced that this time has a huge effect on Greta and our relationship with her. There were particular passages in your ideas that had resonance with me. The idea of "resetting" cortisol levels seems to chime true, as I almost feel a "chemical" change in my mood and hers when we spend time closely engaged together. It is also apparent to me how important this time is, because if we miss it for more than a couple of days or so, I feel our relationship become more distant, and my daughter becomes more truculent, more "needy" and less able to play by herself or with her brother happily. After our charging-up session she can go and do imaginary play, sitting and talking to a doll or teddy bear, explore, read, do whatever she wants independently. As a parent, from a completely selfish point of view, if you give them that time, they will be able to get on with their day without you.

Even a small dose seems to work – maybe it would need more of the 24- or 48-hour approach if the problem was more severe. Our culture is so focused on a reward-and-punishment approach, naughty steps and all the rest of it, that offering a practical alternative is really helpful.'

STORY 16

LB play sessions
Easily distressed: Jeff, aged 4

Jeff is 4 years old and is very attached to his younger sister, Jill, who is 2. They have a younger sister, who is 7 months old. For practical reasons it was not an option for their mother, Carole, to do a 48-hour period away from home, and anyway, she opted to develop her own LB approach.

Jeff's problems

Jeff becomes tremendously distressed by seemingly innocuous events. He cries inconsolably, developing into temper tantrums, deeply upset, almost heartbroken.

When younger, he had extreme reactions to transitions, like having to move out of the parental bed at night or starting nursery school at age 3½. Now he has very emotional reactions when he misinterprets events, more than usually for a 4-year-old. Taken on a preparatory visit for his new school, a teddy bear dressed in the school uniform was shown. Jeff became distraught, believing that the school had stolen his teddy, which had been temporarily lost a few days before (it turned up a few days later). He was crying, shouting, and it took 45 minutes before he calmed down. Similarly, at his swimming lessons, when the teacher had omitted to fill out a form for him, he became very upset. He believed it meant they did not know who he was, that they did not like him, and other incorrect assumptions.

Jeff is very attached to Jill, his younger sister, liking to sleep in the same room with her. He is a nervous boy, prone to catastrophizing seemingly innocuous issues.

The LB play sessions

Two or three times a week, Carole introduced what Jeff named Time In Charge Sessions. These entailed Carole being led in playing by Jeff. She proposed the idea by saying, 'It's Jeff's afternoon: what would you like to do?' Put in control, there was definitely no eating at the dinner table: Jeff asked for jam sandwiches and no set meals. Then he instigated games of various kinds. A basic one was running races, which Mummy had to join in with, holding the baby, charging round the room. However, by far the majority of the time was taken up with fantasy play.

This could entail open-ended scenarios, so that she would get on the floor with him and, for example, imaginary babies would transform into fishes and back again. More commonly, there would be specific narratives that progressed according to his script, sometimes dream-like.

In particular, he enjoyed Disaster scenarios. Carole described one: 'There is a volcano, and we are in a spaceship hurtling towards it. What are we going to do? He would run the story, eventually coming up with the idea of getting a Fire Ship to pour water on the volcano, which caused an explosion that pushed the spaceship off course. Then we would get out of the spaceship via a trampoline, saved. I would say, "Ah, there's this thing called an ejector seat", we'd get it up on the computer and take a look at it.' Another big scenario theme was Fixing Things. There was one where there was a pipe under the road and Jeff had to get a new one, put it in and connect it. Very often the pipe would get broken and he would have to do it all over again. He would be the Foreman, in charge, 'I'm going to direct the repairs', and Carole and her daughters would do the digging. His sister would have a job, even the baby would have one.

Sometimes he would put his sister in charge, but he was still in charge of who was in charge.

The play seems to enable him to get his fears off his chest. Carole recalled that 'He asks a lot of questions about science, and we got him a book. He's obsessed about electricity and wanted to know how it gets from power stations. One time when we were looking at one of these books, he asked, "How do people die?" I said, "It's usually when people are old, their bodies stop working." He asked, "Does that mean Granddad is going to die soon, he's old – or Dad, because he has arthritis?" He was very relieved when I told him it would be alright: "I'm so glad, I've been thinking about it a lot." That was at the end of a very long Time In Charge session. The play makes him feel safe enough to express his deepest fears. It's hugely reassuring for him to put that into words and be told he need not worry.'

Carole did not spend much energy telling him how much she loved him, because she already does that, as well as hugging, a great deal.

The effect of the LB play sessions

Carole reported that 'Immediately after we started the play sessions, the temper tantrums stopped. There were just no incidents any more of a significant nature. That has been true for three months now. If there had been a situation where we said, "Look, we've got to do x or y", before the play sessions he would have had a hysterical reaction. Now he would just accept it or have a proportionate response, perhaps mild disagreement. I would say he was normal, more like my younger daughter. She might get a bit upset and then calm down. He is like that now.'

He behaves differently when away from home as well. 'In the past, people would stare at him as if he is crazy if we were out, very abnormal. We had none of that over the whole summer. He seems to have really benefited from it, he just wanted my intense involvement in these little imaginary worlds.'

The extent of the change in Jeff's whole personality is startling. Says Carole, 'He has been transformed. It took a while, and for a bit I was wondering if it would work, but it certainly has! He now goes to school quite happily, has a good circle of friends, and the extreme emotional behaviour has drastically reduced to the point where it is virtually non-existent. If he does get upset, we can talk him down quite quickly. He is a fantastically loving and intelligent (albeit not conventionally intelligent) boy. He is a joy to be with now and incredibly sensitive to his sisters.'

Two years later

Carole sent me the following report:

> We are doing so much better. I'll tackle my brood from the youngest up.
>
> The youngest is now 2½ and has never experienced me working, so has had full-time hugger Mummy for two-and-a-half years. She is extremely bright, knew over 200 words at 18 months, could count to 15 at 2 years, is very confident within peer groups, and is by far our most confident child, fulfilling the typical family script of a youngest in being the 'risk-taker'. An example is swimming. She happily flings herself into water, completely sure that I will catch her, and, if she goes under the water, comes up laughing at the adventure. She did experience very strong separation anxiety when under 1 year, and would be distraught if separated from me. This has completely disappeared, as we simply responded by letting her stay with me all the time, including at bedtime. She is now confident to be left and has had a few experiences of staying with her Nan as she has 100% one-on-one attention from Nan, and she thrives on this. She's also happy to stay with Dad, and she shares a room with her sister and seems fundamentally emotionally stable (other than the usual temper tantrums of a 2½-year-old, but nothing out of the ordinary).
>
> My middle child, Jill, is now 4 and is also very bright, smiley and confident. When we last corresponded, she had

started nursery, doing 15 hours a week (every morning). We thought that this would be fine, as she was 3½, and based on your earlier book [*How Not to F*** Them Up*], thought that 15 hours wouldn't be too bad. Boy, were we wrong! We suddenly had a very tearful, angry and tired child on our hands where we had had a sweetheart prior to nursery. Some days we had a screaming banshee! We had hardly ever experienced tantrums with her prior to nursery, or many tears. I didn't even discuss it with the nursery – I just complied with the notice period and dropped the sessions by letter. We cut out six hours of nursery provision and replaced it with one-on-one time with Mum, whilst Dad looked after her younger sister. For her Jill In Charge time, she asked for things such as learning the alphabet, writing and drawing, and making cakes. We supplemented this with visits from Granddad, where he spent one-on-one time with her too, which has developed into various rituals like making scrambled eggs together. As if by magic (although, of course, it isn't magic at all) we had our wonderful, affectionate, loving little girl back – within a couple of weeks. It literally went back to how it was before. We have also hooked up with another Mum who is wary of nursery for the under-threes, so we meet up weekly, and my two girls and her girl play together, so she has plenty of socialization with children too. Jill is very good at making friends, and seems ready for school in September, and we feel she will adapt to school really well. There doesn't appear to me to have been any disadvantage academically having that extra time at home; she is already trying to read simple words and is keen to learn. She has swimming and dancing lessons and is very confident in these, even performing on stage in a show without any trepidation. There is absolutely no evidence that her short period of being unhappy about nursery has had any lasting effects, and she is a completely well-adjusted, 'normal' child.

Jeff is an interesting case. Overall, I think that if you put the 3½-year-old Jeff and the 6-year-old Jeff next to each other, you wouldn't recognise them. Jeff was effectively emotionally unmanageable at 3½ and would become distraught over the slightest issue, several times a day; his behaviour was what I considered to be beyond normal parameters. I have an abiding memory of him flailing on the floor screaming and wailing and literally foaming at the mouth because I had said he was going to have his fingernails cut. Another instance occurred when his turn on a bouncy castle had ended, and he was so upset he drew a small crowd of people – they presumably thought we had hurt him in some way. We were unable to attend any form of playgroups or pre-school activities with him, because he simply couldn't conform to whatever the rules of the given activity were. An instance with him attending 'Tumbletots' was a disaster. The room was arranged as a mini assault course with various things to climb on, climb through, jump on etc. – but the 'rule' of the room was you had to move around clockwise, following everyone. A perfectly reasonable rule to avoid total chaos, but this was far too structured for Jeff. He screamed the place down when he was asked to line up, became distraught when moved from one particular climbing frame in an attempt to herd him towards the others, and had such an extreme tantrum we had to go home.

He is now towards the end of Year 1 and has got used to the routine of school. He mixes with other children easily and does not attach himself to one particular friend, so is not a 'dependent' child. School says he is in no way a loner, and, partially due to me being very accommodating, he has lots of friends who come to play at our house regularly. He is confident enough to play at his friends' houses and enjoys it. I feel that if you observed him in the class you wouldn't necessarily be able to distinguish him as having previous extreme emotional problems compared with other children who have had more conventional early babyhoods. He is still sensitive and nervous, so there may still be some remnants of insecurity that we have to iron out. In some situations he is anxious – school assemblies and sports days in particular. He appears self-conscious and does not concentrate on the task in hand as he is preoccupied with people looking at him. So, he appears to lack some confidence and perhaps has a lower self-esteem compared with other children, but this is only manifest in some situations now. School are unconcerned by this and don't consider him to have Special Educational Needs. We are in the process of having these aspects checked out privately with a view to building on the play therapy at home with some drama therapy. We have found a psychodynamic therapist who practises drama, music and art therapy as part of a charity that caters for children who have been bereaved. They will do an assessment of him to see if he would benefit from drama therapy to further build on his progress. I am very determined that he will not grow up to be a future depressive or suffer from anxiety, so we will continue to have Jeff In Charge days and fantasy play (until he doesn't want it any more) and supplement this with drama therapy, if needed.

We have just come back from his 6th birthday party, where 12 of his friends came, and everyone had a wonderful time: no tantrums, no tears, no upsets. Two years ago, I wouldn't have believed this would have been possible. The biggest change in him is that he has become so affectionate with us, spontaneously hugs and kisses us, and responds when we tell him we love him by saying, 'I love you too'.

The key thing that we think has been important is one-on-one time with each of them, when they decide what happens, which takes some juggling and organization with three, but we think it has yielded results. Not forgetting lots and lots of hugs, kisses and fantasy playtime!

WHERE TO GO NEXT IN THE BOOK

Other LB stories that relate to this chapter:

♥ **Two nights away:** Stories 1 (page 27), 2 (page 37), 6 (page 73), 11 (page 126), 17 (page 178) and 18 (page 190)

♥ **One night away:** Stories 3 (page 44), 5 (page 66), 7 (page 86), 8 (page 94) and 20 (page 216)

♥ **Awaydays:** Stories 4 (page 54), 9 (page 104) and 19 (page 213)

♥ **At home:** Story 10 (page 116)

♥ **Spending little or no money:** Stories 8 (page 94), 9 (page 104) and 10 (page 116)

♥ **Children who were born preterm:** Stories 9 (page 104) and 11 (page 126)

♥ **Children aged 3–6:** Stories 2 (page 37), 3 (page 44), 4 (page 54), 5 (page 66) and 9 (page 104)

♥ **Children aged 7–9:** Stories 6 (page 73), 7 (page 86), 8 (page 94), 11 (page 126) and 20 (page 216)

♥ **Children aged 10–13:** Stories 1 (page 27), 10 (page 116), 17 (page 178), 18 (page 190) and 19 (page 213)

♥ **Single parent:** Stories 1 (page 27), 8 (page 94), 10 (page 116) and 19 (page 213)

♥ **Disharmonious relations with a partner:** Stories 1 (page 27), 8 (page 94), 10 (page 116) and 17 (page 178)

TEN

When Love Bombing didn't work

My suspicion is that there are almost no children who would not benefit from Love Bombing, at least to some extent. However, there are circumstances in which either it does not result in any change in the child, or the improvement rapidly disappears.

The stories in this chapter illustrate some of the problems most commonly encountered.

For LB to work, the parent must cede control to the child. Some parents find this either difficult or impossible. In such cases, they will not be able to carry out LB. This is exemplified in the first case in this chapter.

Then there are those situations in which the child's problems are being caused by current difficulties within the family, as when a child is upset by continually witnessing the parents at each other's throats. The second story is an example of this. The little girl concerned benefited considerably from the LB weekend, and her behaviour changing dramatically. Sadly, however, her parents' disharmony continued on their return, and she fell back into her distressed state.

There are also cases where the parent only does LB partially, and it turns into something akin to 'quality time'. Alas, that is not enough, as illustrated by the third story.

Finally, there may be problems that LB cannot touch. For example, in the last story in this chapter, a child has dyspraxia (difficulties with reading and writing), which is immune to LB. In this story, the only one I have encountered, the LB did not, however, affect the difficultness of the child. It is possible that this could be because some children are born with a genetic propensity that is unalterable. However, I do not believe that the evidence supports this idea. In this last case, it is possible that the mother's conviction that her child's destiny was immutable meant that the LB was not done in such a way as to produce change. Many studies show that children whose parents believe that their child's attributes are fixed have worse outcomes than those whose parents believe their child can change – and the same is true of teachers and their pupils.

LB is not a panacea for all childhood problems. I suspect that when its impact is fully researched, it will be shown to work better for some problems than for others. However, I also suspect it will be shown to help almost all children to some extent. The greatest difficulty is not so much the method itself as the parents' capacity and opportunity for carrying it out.

STORY 17

Two nights away
Talented, rebelling against school and underachieving: John, aged 13

Jerri is an enthusiastic, profoundly well-intentioned mother. However, considerable adversity, disharmony with her husband and some kinks in her personality – and let's not forget, we all have them – meant that 13-year-old John was having trouble. The kink is that Jerri is, as she describes herself, a 'control freak', prone to being 'over-controlling' in her dealings with everyone, but especially with John. This limited how much she was able to make LB work.

Jerri was raised in Britain but is married to a German, and they have lived in Germany for over 20 years. They are affluent because both have well-paid jobs.

John's problems

Having been an affectionate, considerate and dutiful son for much of his childhood, John began to worry Jerri when he reached secondary school: 'At night-time he is nervous. He doesn't find it easy to go to sleep and then doesn't sleep well. He does not misbehave at home, but at school he has starting hanging around with the naughty kids. He has started swearing. Above all, where he used to be conscientious about his work, he has disengaged from it.' He is still a voracious reader, but he no longer wants to do his homework or practise hobbies, like the piano.

She believes much of this is because he has witnessed a good deal of arguing at home: 'He has one very good friend whose parents argue like us, and I feel the two boys are comforting each other. I didn't want him in 40 years' time sitting in a psychiatrist's chair stressed by things that had happened long ago. I read your article about Love Bombing, resetting his brain, and I thought, "Right, that's what I'm going to do!"' This proved easier said than done.

The build-up to LB

When I asked Jerri if John had provided a name for the time they were going to have together, she replied, 'Being the control freak, I was the one who would have decided the name, but in fact I decided not to. I just said to him I wanted us to do something together at the weekend. He could choose what we did, when we did it.'

John had difficulty in taking this plan seriously, based on knowledge of his mother. Recalls Jerri, 'Initially, he was very sceptical that I was going to let him choose everything, because that had not been his experience of me. With a tone of disbelief he was saying, "You are going to really let me do what I want?" and I said "Yes". He recognizes that I am a control freak. But after I had repeatedly told him he could decide, then he got a little bit excited about it.' He knew exactly what he wanted to do: visit a town with a mediaeval castle that held fond memories for him. She felt he was hoping to recreate weekends they had had when he was small.

Having raised John's expectations, unfortunately Jerri was then unable to meet them. For a variety of practical reasons, it was not feasible to go to this town; on top of that, John found himself going down with a virus. So Jerri suggested that, as an alternative, they stay 'home alone' for the weekend. Having got John's hopes up, it might have been wiser to simply postpone the weekend, but this did not occur to Jerri. It meant that a basic rule of LB was being broken, in that it was the parent rather than the child who was deciding what was happening, from the outset.

Nonetheless, John was agreeable to the idea, because he hoped that for one weekend he could do anything and everything that he wanted to.

The LB weekend

The Friday night

The Friday night turned out to be a mixed bag. Before they got started, Jerri told John that he had to get his homework and music practice out of the way, so they would not have to worry about it. He went ahead and did it, so he could be completely free.

The problem is that this creates a sense that the LB is having to be earned. Ideally, the child should have no sense that it is a reward. Having to be 'good' preceding the LB is best avoided, so that the child feels that the love and control is not conditional – that he is loved whatever happens, in relation to LB.

The homework out of the way, the LB began, with John deciding he wanted to eat his favourite sausage, followed by lavish helpings of ice cream, as they sat companionably watching his choice of TV programmes until later than his normal bedtime.

The Saturday

A number of activities had been planned, but the weather was cold and inhospitable. John decided he wanted to just stay at home, and Jerri thought, 'Ok, it's his call. There was a little bit of me that thought, "We planned these activities, we should go and do them." But then I thought, "He's choosing not to do them, we're not going to", so we didn't.'

There followed a 'very self-indulgent weekend'. They watched a lot of TV and films, stayed up late together, and Jerri reported 'A very enjoyable, nice time. I felt that we connected. We laughed about things together that we hadn't done for a long while, typical boy things like farting, that I don't usually find funny. I was getting on his wavelength, doing things his way. We cuddled up on the sofa and watched films. We did connect in a way that we have not done for a long time.'

John said he was 'a bit embarrassed' when she praised him, saying that it made him feel uncomfortable and that he was not used to it. He also told her that he finds it distressing that his parents argue so much, and he wishes they would stop. He believes that she changed her behaviour towards him when he started primary school, and it got worse since her father had died when John was 9. Jerri also 'realized how little I tell him that I love him. I did it more when he was small – but I now realize it was not as much as I thought I did.' John was 'very embarrassed' at the beginning of the weekend when she said 'I love you' to him. He said, 'I don't like it when you say that you love me.' He still does not say it to her, but now she thinks he accepts it. One consequence of the weekend is that she does do so more often.

The Sunday

They got up late, and during the morning the intimacy continued, However, by the afternoon Jerri was getting tired and had a 'meltdown'. 'I sometimes ask myself, "Who is the child in this family?" It wasn't really fair to him. I am not going to tell you what the incident was, but it was not really fair on him. We argued really horribly. I am afraid that I did not keep up my end of the bargain to do the Love Bombing as described. I am actually too ashamed to talk about my inappropriate behaviour, and I don't even remember what triggered it, but I probably undid all the good progress. In my moments of (dis)stress, I forget everything and behave very inappropriately, shouting, screaming, threatening to leave. I am afraid of setting up a pattern with him which is similar to that with my husband – lots of shouting, screaming and then making up and saying sorry.'

After her 'meltdown', the LB component of the weekend was abandoned.

The LB Top-Ups

Not having a name for the LB experience nor any objects to symbolize the experience made it harder to have Top-Ups. Those reminders seem important in triggering the idea that parent and child can enter the LB zone in which the normal rules are suspended. That the LB weekend had ended so fractiously did not help either. You might have supposed Jerri would just have abandoned the whole idea. But she showed her commitment to improving matters by not giving up. From time to time they would spend an LB evening, with John doing what he wants, watching what he wanted on TV and eating what he wanted.

What was more, Jerri decided to try to have another stab at time away with John, albeit her own version of LB. A few months later, to get away from the mournful atmosphere at home created by the approaching death of her mother-in-law from cancer, she told John she was taking him to Berlin for a week's respite.

Whilst presenting it in this way – her decision, he had no choice – was not creating an LB experience, she did try to incorporate some of the elements. She decided without consultation where they stayed, but she did give him choices about where and what they did, and about meals. He ended up liking a really nice Italian restaurant, which they went to three times. Her response was, 'Ok, we'll go there.' She did propose activities, but she did not give instructions as to which to choose. She presented John with choices and asked what he would like.

Perhaps most significantly, she was able to have patches in which she could relate to him as she had in the past. 'I learnt if I talked to him nicely and calmly – the little things I used to do when he was young to jolly him along – I have much more success.' For brief periods, she was able to be adult and to let him depend on her and even regress to a younger age, a vital component of the LB technique. As she put it, 'I was able to talk to him without that demanding, nagging tone in my voice, and he would become like the loveable child I used to know.'

The week did not pass without tensions. On one occasion, he wanted to eat at McDonalds. As a vegetarian, she found that hard to take and 'sat there sulking', resulting in him 'having a bit of a meltdown'.

Nonetheless, she recognized that the LB components that she was able to tolerate did improve their relationship at the time.

The effects of the LB

Jerri summarized the impact of the various LB attempts as follows: 'I would say it was a tempered success. We talk more and communicate better, but only when I remember to talk calmly. I really would like to do the Love Bombing properly, but this requires better mental preparation on my part. I have discovered that the way I talk to John makes a big difference to how receptive he is to what I say, and it is something that I do have to do consciously. He is also more secure when I talk calmly to him, but my family dynamics are not normally that way. We still argue; the main difference is that we are aware of how much we do so, and we talk more and are more forgiving.'

John's behaviour is still the same. What benefits there have been, if any, seem to have been in Jerri's relationship with John.

However, Jerri recognizes that much of the problem of making LB work for John lay in her own personality. She says, 'The poor guy had just been getting a lot of grief from me about how his school marks weren't what they used to be and me shouting at him. He was pretty defensive, quite rightly. He still says that he's not quite sure that he trusts me because he doesn't know which way the wind is going to blow. I find that very sad. In a way, I made that bed and I must lie in it. I hope that one day he will be able to say that Mum will do what she claims she will do and not have a meltdown.'

She is determined to try to change herself, and still believes that LB could work if she were less controlling. 'Doing it properly might shift his conviction that he can't trust me to let him have control. The problem is not with him, it's with me. I haven't been able to do it properly because it's like everything in my life: I do things, but not very well. I do them, but not completely, so you don't get the real benefits of it. I pretend to do it.'

The impact of John being a teen on whether LB can help

Part of the difficulty of doing LB with teenagers is that they are often engaged in trying to become independent of their mother. Writing to me two years after she did the LB, Jerri says, 'I recognize he is trying to cut the apron strings. He is now 14, and there's things I am not allowed to do. If I want to muss up his hair or tickle his feet, it can only happen if he allows me to do it.' However, the problem is exacerbated in this case by Jerri's insecurities. She admits that 'I do find it hard to let go. I am trying to make him younger than he is. I don't think that's really fair on him. One of the things we used to do was to go together to the movies as a family. Then his father could not come, and just John and I went. This last year he just doesn't want to do it with me any more. That really upsets me.' She acknowledges that she is using John as an antidote to loneliness. 'I admit I find it upsetting to imagine being away from John for any length of time. I am dependent on him: that poisons your relationship.' These factors seem more important than John's age in explaining how the LB turned out and its lack of an effect on him.

There is also the problem that even on the occasions when Jerri is calm and able to let him be, her past behaviour makes it hard for John to accept the possibility that she will not be controlling and will not melt down. Jerri comments that 'I am a lot more laid back than I used to be, but he assumes that I am trying to control him when I am not. If I make suggestions, he is not keen to take them on board, cutting off his own nose to spite his face. For example, we are a family that reads a lot, with many books. If there is an author he likes, I will buy him books by that person because I know what his tastes are, but he will refuse to read them just because I have got them for him. It's a case of "I didn't choose it, so I'm not going to read it." It's a bit sad.' Again, these problems should not be conflated with the fact that John is in his teens.

John's childhood history

Jerri had several miscarriages before John was born. She was thrilled when she managed to carry him through to birth, and felt that he was an adorable baby. However, from four weeks after the birth on, she suffered a depression that went on for several years. Although she 'loved him to bits', she felt that she never bonded with him, spending 'hours looking into his eyes' but 'never really feeling a good connection with him'. An architect by training, she returned to work at the first opportunity, when John was 4 months, her elderly in-laws taking over the care of him. At 9 months he moved into a workplace crèche, where he was dropped off each morning at 9 a.m. and collected by her in-laws at 3 p.m.

There were tensions between her and the in-laws because she felt they ignored her many injunctions as to how John should be cared for. A vegetarian, she was upset that they fed him meat.

There were also cultural clashes. She felt that it was three against one: her in-laws and husband against her.

When her mother-in-law developed cancer, her husband – an only child – was deeply distressed, and their arguments became florid. His parents were calm and easy-going, on the whole, and he found her control-freakery hard to bear. He also worked very long hours, leaving her alone for much of the time. Following couple counselling, he decided to stay with her, but their tumultuous arguments began to be witnessed by John when he ceased spending so much time at Jerri's in-laws', following her mother-in-law's illness. Jerri says that 'there was a lot of shouting in our house. It did make him anxious, because he feared we would break up – no child wants that – and he has had to put up with adult relationships before he was ready. What I say to him is that I am very sorry, I can't turn back the clock.'

The arguments had been going on from early in John's life. Jerri recalls that 'We were all in our little corners, and the only thing that was keeping us together was this lovely little baby. He was a very good baby, then as a toddler very well-behaved, very kind.' It may well be that John developed a compliant and caring component to his character very early in life, feeling that he had to look after his depressed and furious mother. He may also have sought to be the diplomat between his warring parents to whom he frequently said that he was scared they would break up.

It seems that John was required to do a lot of caring for Jerri. She has also transmitted some of her problems to him. John is concerned that he has a psychotic illness. Sometimes he responds to what she says with 'I'm not mad Mum, I'm not mad.' She believes that 'He is scared I will send him to psychiatrists and, to be honest, in the past I have warned that that will happen, I have said, "If we do not sort ourselves out, it's what will happen."' This sucks John into her feeling of being mad and needing help and draws him into the disharmonious marriage. He was 'a very understanding child' until about the age of 9 or 10, and then he began to say, 'You can't tell me these things.' She says, 'I don't think I ever told him inappropriate things, but there were some things he just didn't really want to know. I realized I was confiding in him when I shouldn't have been.' This suggests that she was involving him in her problems at an age when John could not cope with them. She comments that 'The good thing was, it was the child who realized that, not me', but, of course, that ignores the fact that it would have been better for John if he had not been involved at all.

Today, she says, her husband 'is used to my histrionics, I can be a bit of a drama queen. John has learnt to disengage himself when that happens, like his father did. If I start screaming or shouting, they just ignore me, which only makes me worse.' Depressed people are often highly aggressive towards their intimates, even though to others they may seem quiet, passive and withdrawn. In addition, people who are insecure about whether others can be relied upon to meet their needs and do their bidding are very easily upset and angered by those they depend on. The depression and insecurity often go together, and both can result in aggressive behaviour in relationships.

Her fears get expressed in perfectionism and a constant need to control what others are doing. Jerri says, 'I have this great need to control outcomes, but you can't really control things.' In relation to John, apart from a long list of dietary restrictions, she was intrusively concerned about the minutiae of his life. Some of the concerns were ones that have a rational basis, like a desire to protect him from upsetting and inappropriate film and television programmes. But a great many of her interventions with him entailed micro-management of his activities, which left him no autonomy.

Jerri is well aware that her difficulties date back to her own childhood. She refused to take antidepressant medication, so has had some therapy, from which she has gained considerable insight. She was the youngest of four children in a 'noisy', 'argumentative' family home. She alludes to there having been 'some pretty traumatic things' that happened to her, and she is aware that whenever she got too close to remembering them in therapy, she would run away.

Having said all this, there appear to have been two important components of John's childhood that may have provided him with resilience. One is that, early on in his life, his father and his father's parents were able to tune in to him and give him the love that Jerri felt but found it so hard to give. This provides an internal security, the sense that things can be alright. John's relationship with his father provides a barrier against his mother's intrusiveness. Fortunately, this is something she is able to tolerate, even to encourage, showing how well-intentioned she is and how insightful she can be.

Knowing that her husband might be put off if she bombarded him with her enthusiasm with the idea of LB, she decided 'not to make it me telling him what to do. I just said, "be nice and kind to him".' They went away for four days and returned apparently having agreed that she is hard to handle. 'They seem to have had issues with me and my control-freakery.' She says of John, 'I am quite optimistic how he will turn out, but also that he might get depressed, be anxious, be lonely, almost the things that I worry about for myself that I am transferring onto him, which is not right.' This may well be true and is another sign of her considerable intelligence. If she has used him as a dustbin for these distressed aspects of herself, they may be easier for him to disentangle than severe early deprivation or abuse would be, of the kind that she may have suffered.

Indeed, for all her difficulties, Jerri is the other positive component in John's childhood. Whilst she could not bond with him early on, she has poured a lot of love into him subsequently, not all of it for selfish reasons. As she puts it, 'Being an only child, it was "Mummy entertainment" all the time. I did things with him, I played with him – you don't see many 40-year-olds jumping on the trampoline!' His creativity and sharp mind may well be the consequence of this shared play.

Jerri has had to struggle against great odds. Her childhood contained considerable maltreatment, she was living in a foreign culture, illness plagued her and her relatives, and she had a fraught, disharmonious relationship with her husband. For all that, she is determined to do her best to help her son. Her plan is to sort herself out as soon as possible through further therapy and then to do her best to show John that she can give him a different experience. It is not too late for her to do that.

STORY 18

Two nights away
Made nervy and angry by parents rowing: Mary, aged 10

Mary, 10, is the youngest of three daughters. Her parents are called Ella and Tim. Unfortunately, there has been considerable tension in the marriage, which Ella believes is the primary cause of Mary's problems.

Ella and Tim work together as partners in a firm of solicitors in a city in the West of England. Their two other daughters are both older than Mary: one aged 18, Maddy, from a previous marriage, and Gemma, aged 12.

When Love Bombing didn't work

This was a sad story, in that the LB was a great success but its benefits were soon destroyed when they got home by the destructive relationship between Ella and Tim.

Mary's difficulties

When Ella first contacted me, she summarized Mary's problems as follows:

> She gets extremely distressed by any sign of conflict and is overly anxious about whether it will happen. For example, she is concerned that we will argue if we are left alone. She checks every night at bedtime whether we are staying up together and, if so, whether we will be in the same room.
>
> She behaves well at school but is impatient, aggressive and very argumentative at home. At bedtime, she has sweaty palms, is scared. Ostensibly, she is the daughter most badly affected by our disharmony.

At the worst moments during the rancour between Mary's parents, she has said that she hates herself and wants to die.

The fears become most pronounced at night, when she is terrified of being in a room alone. Going to bed, she is scared that a stranger will climb through her window and snatch her away.

Preparing for the LB weekend

Ella is a sensible, thoughtful and organized person, so she was careful to pick a weekend that she knew would be succeeded by at least a couple of weeks in which she would be able to do the Top-Ups because Tim would be able to help out in the evenings. She was also careful to avoid creating tensions with her other daughters, aware that they might feel left out. As we shall see,

Ella was also highly skilled and sensitive in allowing Mary to feel in control.

Being reasonably prosperous, Ella could afford to take Mary away for a weekend at a bed & breakfast (B&B) in St Ives, a Cornish holiday resort where they had been before and of which Mary has fond memories. Mary had opted for this plan very quickly, and there was much talking about the weekend and a big build-up. Having recently got into doing Internet research, Mary avidly explored places to stay.

She opened a folder on the computer with the name 'Mary and Mummy's Special Time', and when Ella noticed it, she asked if that was the name she wanted to give to the weekend. Ella was wary of saying this in a way that pressurized Mary, who confirmed that yes, this was her chosen title. She explained that she had not called it Mummy Time because she did not want her father to feel left out. In due course, the experience became known as Special Time, as shorthand.

The LB weekend

The first night

While waiting for the train at the station, Mary asked to look for some DVDs in a shop. One of her reasons for choosing the B&B was that it had a DVD player in the room, so she was looking forward to time spent watching films together. The shop had some '3 for £10' selections, from which Ella let her choose.

This LB case is unusual in that, although they were not rich, it was usually affordable for Ella to let her daughter buy things that she wanted: there was some spare money in the budget because the B&B was a cheap one. It is also an interesting illustration of how it can be healthy and helpful to allow the child to feel in control by acceding to his wishes to spend money. Whilst there is always a risk of parents creating a false equation between love and money when in the LB zone, if affordable such expenditure can be used by the child to give himself a strong sense of autonomy and control, which is highly beneficial.

Another reason Mary had chosen this accommodation was that it offered breakfast in bed. Once settled in their room, she loved filling out the form beside the bed ordering what she wanted, ticking the fruit juices, croissants and so forth.

From the beginning, Ella was remarkably sensitive to the issue of control. The breakfast-in-bed issue had nearly led to a problem during the planning stage because Mary preferred a hotel to the B&B, on the grounds that it did breakfast in bed. In fact, she had muddled them up. Ella suggested she check on the computer when she saw this, but Mary wanted to do something else at that moment. Instead of insisting she check it there and then, as she normally would have, Ella said, "Okay, maybe take a look at it later", and that is what happened.

Mary loves her food, and a couple of nice meals were part of the plan. On arrival, the B&B proprietor suggested a little Italian restaurant two doors away. Ella had brought some pencils and pens, with paper, as usually they play Hangman or Noughts and Crosses while waiting for food. However, recently Mary has been getting into quiz magazines. Using a pictogram, she created a sentence, which she asked her mother to guess. Decoded, it said, 'I am really looking forward to having time with you.'

This was typical of Mary, Ella says, because 'She's quite shy about volunteering what she feels. In the family group, if she wants to say something, quite often she will want to whisper it. She feels exposed if it's too open and spelt out. I don't know if it's the right thing to do, but I say, "Just tell us what's on your mind." In the family group she will say, "I will tell Mum first", almost as a preparation: it's not that she wants to keep it a secret.

She wasn't as much like that when she was younger, before she witnessed the rows between Tim and me. Re-watching the family videos, I am very struck by how much more relaxed all the girls looked in the past, at ease with one another.'

Mary is not a pudding person. As soon as the main course had been eaten, she wanted to go back to the B&B and watch the first DVD, which they did.

In the room, Ella could tell that Mary was nervous because there was a fire-escape ladder near the window, and she was worrying that there was someone on it. However, they did not discuss it then, and cuddled up together in the bed and fell happily asleep.

The Saturday

Mary wanted to set an alarm so that they would be ready when the breakfast came. She was wobbly about the idea of a stranger walking in when she was in her pyjamas, so they woke at 8 am. Ella felt they had 'a most lovely time' watching *Tracy Beaker* and other children's TV in bed, 'completely flopping and cuddling up'.

As they got closer to the hour that breakfast was expected, Mary kept asking what time it was. When the knock on the door finally came, she jumped out of bed and ran into the little bathroom: she did not want to be there when they came in.

This problem navigated, she loved her breakfast in bed. Mary has very adult tastes: she likes coffee and tea and strong cheeses, even the taste of alcohol. She has always felt very self-conscious about liking those things. If in a restaurant, she will ask Ella to order it for herself, because she does not want to draw attention to the fact that it's for a child. In this case, she did not want the waiter to know she had ordered the tea. But that was fine, and she relished the breakfast.

After that she wanted to watch a *Tracy Beaker* that had been first shown on Friday night while they were travelling. She had looked at the TV menu and decided that it would be after watching that that they would get up and go out. As soon as it was over, Mary was in a huge hurry. She had planned to go to the market and would not let Ella take a shower. Ella says Mary has a very low patience threshold when she really wants to do something. However, Ella felt this was a different 'let's get going' from at home. It was more that she just wanted to get on with the plan, rather than that she could not bear to be thwarted and delayed. Ella thought, 'Fine, go with the momentum of the day, so we just got up and got out.'

They had a good time wandering round the little lanes and markets. There had been one thing Ella had suggested on the train on the way which turned out to be prescient. Mary loves body lotions and potions and massages on her neck. Ella had brought some Body Shop lotion and nail varnish, saying that if they felt tired and floppy, they could just do that in the B&B room. Mary is not very 'girly', but she had been intrigued once when her mother went to have her legs waxed before going on holiday and saw someone having her nails painted in the salon. Mary had asked several times for it, but Ella had felt it would not be right, never having had a manicure in her life, let alone as a 10-year-old.

Hence, when Ella saw a shop offering manicures in St Ives, she thought 'why not?' There was no one there, and, as luck would have it, the manicurist was sitting with her own 10-year-old daughter whom she was about to paint. So they both had it done, with the girl suggesting colours and giving Mary suggestions, like that she could have flower shapes on the nails. Ella commented, 'That was really nice: something I knew she wanted to do, able to give her a treat.' It was a loving present as well as a way of making Mary feel in control.

After that they just wandered round the streets a bit longer, ending up in some mainstream chain shops where Mary bought a couple of T-shirts. They had takeaway fish 'n' chips because Mary wanted to keep wandering rather than sit down. She was determined to keep walking. It was fortunate they had had a sit-down in the manicurist or they might have been exhausted.

The great thing, Ella said, was that Mary felt enabled to insist on what she wanted. Mary kept on doing things that she knows Ella would normally say no to, like leaving without a shower, or choosing which cardigan her mother should wear, as well as the purchases. Ella was able just to say 'fine', the empowerment and control was there.

Ella also said 'I love you' to her a lot, and Mary said she loved her back. It's something they do anyway, but Ella pointed out that 'Some of it is habit and mechanical, and this time I made sure it wasn't like that. I realized I never actually looked her in the eye while doing it.' She was not sure when to do that, trying to let it happen when it seemed natural.

By now it was early evening, and they bought a few snacks that Mary likes. She chose foods like satsumas, olives and hou-mous, and they took them back to the B&B. They set them up on a table in the dining room, and that was when Mary said she did not want to go out again. She had scheduled for them to set off in the dark for the funfair on the seafront because she thought that would be exciting. Instead, she said, 'Let's have lovely fun here. I feel tired, let's go there tomorrow', but then nervously asked, 'Do you mind if we don't?' She was worried Ella would say they had to stick to the plan, which normally she might have. Ella said 'Fine', realizing that Mary had the sense that she had both made and changed the plan and was really in charge.

After eating, they went to their room and watched the sec-ond DVD. One of the things she had bought while wandering around was a book of *Snoopy* cartoons. So, after the film, they snuggled up and read that. They had 'lots of cuddly time'.

However, as the moment approached to go to sleep, Mary said, 'You know those noises? It sounds like there's somebody on the ladder.' Ella explained it was the wind, that this was a rattling, old Victorian house, with gurgling pipes: it was not someone outside who wanted to come in. Mary seemed to accept that quite quickly, probably, Ella said, 'Because she was feeling loved and safe and had been in control all day. She accepted it much more readily than if we had spent the day normally. I reassured her a couple of times, and she volunteered a few minutes later that she wasn't scared any more.'

The Sunday

Because they couldn't have the full cooked breakfast in the bedroom, Mary wanted to go down for it. So they got up at 9.30, this time with Ella being permitted a shower while Mary chose their clothes. Downstairs, she was the only child in the dining room, with couples at the other tables. She felt a little conspicuous. She would not order tea, something a child might not request, but otherwise she relaxed. There was a little computer for guest use, and the manicurist had suggested a Jamie Oliver restaurant. While waiting for breakfast to come, Ella looked at its menu on the Internet.

It was a nice day, sunny and not too cold, but windy. After breakfast, Mary wanted to walk along the front where there are lots of little souvenir shops. She wanted something for her Dad and two sisters. She had already put doing this on the list of activities she wanted: specifically, sweets in wraps from a traditional sweet shop she knew. They had already been purchased on the Saturday, but now she bought a couple of little shells and a stick of rock for the other family members, expressing her constant concern to keep everyone sweet. This had been evident from the start. The first thing she had wanted to do on the Friday night was to make a little video of the room on Ella's phone and send it home. On Sunday morning, her middle sister called and spoke to her for a little bit, which was fine.

Finally, they reached the funfair, a high point in Ella's plan. Although Ella is generally fearful, she is fearless about actual physical danger. At school she is in the trapeze club and, much braver than her sister, will fling herself off anything from a great height. At funfairs she is first in the queue for the scary rides. Ella does not normally go on them, but part of the deal was that Ella would go on any ride Mary chose.

Unfortunately, the biggest rollercoaster only ran if there were 12 people for the car. On a Sunday morning this was hard to arrange. They stood there for a bit, chatting, waiting patiently for enough people. Normally, Ella says, 'She would be impatient, but on this occasion she was quite calm. It was noticeable that she didn't lose control and get distressed.' The wait went on for some time, until, eventually, Ella suggested they try another ride and then come back. There was another, albeit tamer, one next-door.

Ella comments: 'I have to say, I'm now a rollercoaster convert! There was a high wind, and we went in a car with a couple. I was laughing and screaming hysterically. Mary would normally be embarrassed by that, but she seemed glad I had enjoyed it.'

They returned to the big rollercoaster, but it was still no good, so they went on an octopus machine instead. Returning yet again to the big rollercoaster, there was still no dice, so they headed for the smaller rollercoaster again. As they approached it, Mary said, 'Don't scream and laugh so loudly, Mummy.' Ella thought, 'Okay, I will control myself.' This time there were two young teenage girls sharing with them, and after a few rounds Ella couldn't restrain herself. The teenagers had been quiet up to that point, but they started screaming too. Afterwards, Mary seemed happy with Ella when Ella raised the screaming. Normally, it could have spoiled the experience for her.

They had yet another look at the large rollercoaster, but still no luck. Ella commented: 'What was good was, she didn't get frustrated, despite being persistent.' Instead, they went on the bumper cars. Mary had driven one before. She liked being at the controls, spinning round, in charge.

Finally, they proceeded to the amusement arcade. Every year she would have a go on the machine with the arm that comes down and grabs a teddy. Ella had always told her it's very unlikely a bear will be picked up, the machine is configured to fail. Amazingly, just as they arrived, a man had actually picked one up. They put in enough money for three goes, and on the second Mary picked a dog up, but the arm dropped it, for no good reason, the machine jamming. The supervisor was called and was also unable to make it work. Usually, Mary would have been embarrassed by Ella persisting and Ella was worried it was all going to go wrong, but Mary did not seem worried: she was 'just watching, not agitated'. Eventually, the supervisor opened up the machine and gave them the dog. Recalls Ella, 'It was perfect. After years of trying to get one, she had succeeded! Without any meltdown or impatience, it had come right.'

After that they bought £1 in 2p pieces for the machine that gradually shoves the coins over a shelf. She put some coins down on the shelf to try to get some back, remaining absorbed by it for a long time. At the end, she was quite happy to finish, ready to leave, clutching her dog, to set off for the Jamie Oliver restaurant.

Going there, Mary got a little frustrated by roadworks block-ing the way, unable to see how far they extended round a corner, getting stuck on a traffic island. She got momentarily angry, then immediately checked herself, uncharacteristically recognizing that she had shouted at Ella, and then apologizing.

At the restaurant, for which bookings could not be made, there was half an hour's wait. Whilst they were waiting, Mary spotted a cookery book that she wanted to give as a present to Tim for his birthday. She was happy to just look at the menu. They had half-size portions for children, which was perfect for her, even though she has a big appetite. She does not like dumbed-down kids' food, so she could have adult food.

As soon as she had finished her main course, not being a pudding person she said, 'Let's just go now. I'm ready to set off home.' Their bags were packed at the B&B. Mary said she was tired, so Ella suggested they order a taxi to the station. Mary went on the computer and found the number for one. They waited 10 minutes for it to arrive, with Mary playing on the computer.

This being Sunday, there were engineering works being done on the rails, and they had to get a bus for some of the journey. Normally, before a journey Mary would ask nervously about the minutiae of how each leg will be done, how long it will take, but not on this occasion. Ella thought Mary might find it difficult as the bus was something unexpected, but she was fine with it.

On the train journey they read the *Snoopy* book. These have become 'a big thing'. 'It's Charlie Brown, but the dog is personified in about nine different ways. One is all about him being a barrister, another is him as a Red Baron World War One flying ace, Scout Leader and so on, giving different views of the world. Mary was fascinated by them, so we got lots more, and whenever there's "down-time" we settle down with them. She carries the one we bought in the market with her to school every day in her bag, even though it's quite a chunky book. They are allowed to read for half an hour every day, so she reads it then. I don't know if that's a reminder of the experience or she just likes the book, or a bit of both.'

Tim had texted, offering a lift from the station. In the event, with the changes to the timetable due to the engineering works, he had thought they would be later than they were, so they had to wait 5 minutes for him at the pick-up point at the station. Mary was getting tired by then and just wanted to be home. Ella reported that 'She got a little bit fractious, "Where's Daddy, why are we waiting?", a bit grumpy, but really only momentarily. Previously, that would have built up to her getting more and more distressed, winding herself up into "I want to go NOW", worrying which direction he was going to come from. Her normal reaction would be an aggressive, petulant irritation, her tone of voice high-pitched and demanding, but none of that happened. A couple of minutes later he arrived, and it was all easy.'

When they got home, supper proceeded smoothly. Mary was a bit disappointed that the family did not have a greater reaction to the presents, but she did not worry excessively.

A bit later, upstairs, Ella was in the bathroom when she heard Mary ask Tim to get something from her bag, and he said 'no', he was not on his way downstairs. Mary would usually not want to go down on her own at that hour, partly because there would be no one else down there, and partly because when she asks someone to do something, if she is tired, she will get aggressively impatient at being thwarted. Ella was thinking, 'Oh oh, here we go', but it was fine, Mary just went down and got it. Ella commented, 'That seems like a tiny thing. But it showed a massive difference. There was no fuss because no fears or feeling that she was being let down.'

Mary likes to know who's going to be putting her to bed and who will be taking her to school and picking her up the next day. Because the parents alternate, this varies. But on this night Mary said, 'I'm going up to bed. Come up in ten minutes', off her own bat, without asking which of them would be coming or about the arrangements for the next day. Said Ella, 'That was the first time she had ever done that. It's never been her volunteering to do it, always us saying, "Now it's time." Either she would then insist one of us come or would cling to her sister and get her to come. To volunteer AND to do it without her sister was a big thing.'

The Top-Ups

In the succeeding week, the Top-Ups were a very relaxed mix of drawing cartoons together, reading, cuddling and chatting. The greatest difficulty was in dealing with Mary's sisters' understandable desire for attention when Tim was not also there.

For example, one evening Ella had been drawing cartoons with Gemma (the middle daughter). As it was getting close to bedtime, Ella suggested that she and Mary go to her room for the half-hour Special Time. Gemma came in about 10 minutes later, and Ella asked her to give them 15 minutes alone, which she accepted. She was leaving when Mary asked whether Gemma could stay and draw with them. Ella said matter-of-factly that this was their half-hour Special Time and she would really like it to be time like they had at the weekend. Both girls seemed to 'get' that straight away, with no problems.

The effects of the LB

There was a marked change in the days succeeding the LB weekend in the extent and manner of Mary's aggression in the family and in her attitude to night-times.

The day after the LB weekend, Monday, was a bit of a 'kit-heavy' day for Mary. She had got her music and PE stuff to

collect together and carry. She needed help carting it all downstairs and shouted down to Ella, but she was cooking porridge.
Ella yelled up for her to bring one thing down now, and she
would help after breakfast. Mary started shouting – not a massive tantrum, just 'I want some help' – then it went quiet and
she carried everything downstairs, just got on with it. This was,
according to Ella, 'uncharacteristic, to say the least'.

The next morning was straightforward. However, that
evening, after supper, Mary and her eldest sister, Maddy, had
an argument, the first since returning from the LB weekend.
Maddy had dropped some food in Mary's water whilst reaching
over to serve herself. Mary asked to swap glasses, but Maddy
refused and challenged Mary, saying she had asked too rudely.
This is one of Maddy's ongoing complaints. Whether Mary had
been rude or not, what interested Ella is that after she asked
them both to calm down so they could all eat, Mary stopped
straight away, whereas previously she would almost certainly
have lost control.

A positive of this exchange was that Ella was able subsequently to take Maddy aside and ask her to 'cut Mary some
slack' for a few days. Ella had been concerned from the outset
that the LB would create jealous friction. Mary's sisters are on
the lookout for signs that their mother does not come down
as hard on her as she does on them. The positive was that
Maddy was able to see that Mary is an anxious girl, to get a
sight of her point of view, and then to be less annoyed by her
rudeness.

However, on the Thursday an acrimonious dispute broke out
between Mary and Gemma after school, ending in blows. Ella
took Mary up to her room and reminded her of what a great
time they had had during their Special Time, and she quickly
calmed down. Ella was impressed by how quickly Mary regained
control. They went out to the shops together to get some food.

Again Mary became a bit grumpy, but again she pulled herself up and remarked that she had not reacted well, and apologized. They recalled the LB weekend again.

In succeeding weeks the improvement continued. To this point, Ella concluded that there had been several important changes caused by the LB and the Top-Ups.

The first was that Mary was less reactive and impatient. On the occasions when she did get angry, she seemed to be much better able to soothe herself, so the aggressive outbreaks were both less extreme and less protracted. She was also much less worried about being alone at night, either downstairs or upstairs.

The second impact was on Ella's own behaviour. She was finding it easier to let Mary's everyday minor negative behaviour go and to respond positively and calmly to her. She feels LB is a two-way process in adjusting emotional thermostats, the mother's as well as the child's. Indeed, she went so far as to wonder if it is primarily the parent's thermostat that needs adjusting. She feels that she is better able to identify with Mary's predicament and break the pattern of seeing all negative behaviour as an indication of a major crisis. Like so many mothers, she has some guilt about her daughter, and she felt that the LB had to some extent liberated her from it, making her less likely to overreact if Mary seemed distressed.

She feels that, in asking the parent to tell her child you love him, you are helping him remind himself how much he really does too. In that respect, she concluded, 'It's a fantastic two-way process.'

Sadly, this progress was ultimately sabotaged by the relationships with the family (see below), but it did last for a couple of months. The trouble was that Ella and Tim were unable to sort out their relationship.

The causes of Mary's distress

The foundations of Mary's distress may have been in her earliest years, in that Ella found it hard to tune in to Mary in the first months. The pregnancy and birth had gone swimmingly, but afterwards she found herself feeling detached and 'a bit down'. Ella describes herself as 'a complete career machine', and after the birth of all her children was eager to return to work as soon as possible.

However, she was able to find a child-minder, effectively a nanny, who looked after both Mary and Maddy through their early years. She feels this minder was a warm person who gave them well-organized and child-centred care. Her only reservation is that the minder may have lacked empathy, was a pragmatic, somewhat inflexible and hard person at times.

Whatever the importance of these speculations, there is little doubt that Mary was considerably unsettled by the long history of disharmony between her parents.

Ella and Tim got together after her first husband had abandoned the family soon after Maddy's birth. Tim and Ella worked in the same office. All three daughters have been exposed in different ways to the rancour, but its nature, says Ella, 'has changed quite dramatically over the last few years'.

Ella had always made a huge effort not to argue with Tim in front of the children, as she is one of six siblings and had grown up surrounded by continual conflict. At the time, she had thought she was managing to hide the conflict from them.

She felt abandoned by the extent to which Tim was absent, both literally, as he worked seven days a week, and emotionally, in that he was self-absorbed and disengaged when he was actually at home. During their rare times together in the evening, if she raised how she felt with him, she has since realized it was usually in an overly aggressive and challenging way. He would walk out and refuse to discuss it.

Being in the same profession and office, she understood the pressures but found it hard to accept the sense of being 'conned'. Tim had been aware of her past bad relationship and had portrayed himself as wanting to commit to a life together as companion and parent. Previously, when she was with her first husband, he had been both her colleague and her friend.

During the early years, Tim would occasionally have what he called a 'red mist' in front of the children, completely out of control and using very violent language directed at himself, phrases like 'Why don't you get a knife and stab me?' He was never physically violent, and whenever this happened, Ella would stay in a state that, in retrospect, she describes as 'almost overly calm, as if a switch had gone off inside me that prevented me arguing back or retaliating in any way, in order to protect the children as much as I could. I am one of six children and would normally stand my ground and argue back, so this was quite surprising, it almost happened automatically.' There may have been an element of disembodiment about this reaction, revisiting a detachment that she may have developed in response to the strife in her original family.

During the pregnancy with Mary, she persuaded Tim to go for marriage guidance counselling to explore how they could communicate better and find a way to discuss their feelings without them becoming a source of conflict. They entered a programme of six weekly sessions, which Tim spent dismissing the concerns she raised and claiming that his life was great and he could not see the problem. They stopped after the fifth session, as it seemed so pointless.

The communication between them did not improve. Whenever a difficulty arose, they had no way of effectively discussing it, so most issues just festered. As stresses built up at work and at home, the only time they spent together as a couple entailed arguing, even in restaurants, even when celebrating an anniversary. About four years earlier, when Mary was aged 6, Tim decided that he wanted to try counselling again and arranged sessions to which they went weekly for two and a half years.

Ella found she was becoming more and more depressed during this time. Gradually she decided that this was because, instead of the counselling helping to resolve their communication issues, the session was becoming a kind of absolution for Tim: he saw it as having done his bit for the week, and there was no attempt to address their life outside the consulting room. To compound that, Tim continued to say in many sessions that Ella seemed happy enough day to day, or that they had just had 'a really lovely weekend' with friends, or 'a lovely holiday' with the kids. He said this even though she had tried to explain to him that she was acting, to protect the children, as she did not want to fight in front of them. He could not accept that there was much wrong, even though she was only pretending to be calm and enjoying the family time.

Ella was so frustrated with the process that she stopped going to counselling, although Tim continued. Critically, at the same time she decided to act as she truly felt, to show Tim the reality, even in front of the children. This generated an extremely disharmonious atmosphere where the children were constantly expecting an argument. Both Tim and Ella picked each other up on every little petty thing, so all day, every day, felt like a battle. This, a rancorous family, was the situation at the point when Ella contacted me.

Ella believed that her daughters had reacted differently to it.

Maddy tries to point out what they are doing wrong and tells them they are being bad parents and negatively influencing the younger two (which, Ella believes, 'is clearly true'). Ella suspects it is no coincidence that Maddy has now decided to study psychology at university.

Gemma tries to calm the situation down and make peace, even though she gets quite distressed herself.

Mary gets extremely distressed by any sign of conflict and is overly anxious about whether conflict may happen. There is some element of imitation of angry scenes between the parents. There is fear of her parents disappearing, of the family falling apart. When angry, both parents are emotionally unavailable to her. This leaves a mixture of wanting to protect and console upset parents, but also anger, a feeling of 'What about me?'

There is persuasive scientific evidence that children vary considerably in how they respond to persistent parental rows. In general, many studies show that children of disharmonious parents are more likely to display symptoms of what are known as 'externalizing' problems, like screaming and shouting, fighting, disobedience and delinquency. Obviously, this is partly because if you keep seeing your parents behave that way, you do too.

But not all children of rowing parents react like that. A recent study shows why this might be. Children exposed to repeated parental conflict have been shown to react physically. Their heart rates, the sweatiness of their hands, their sleep patterns and their cortisol levels (the hormone that is secreted to put us into a state of readiness for fight or flight when feeling threatened) are all affected. However, the new study examined more sophisticated bodily reactions.

Our physical responses to the environment are primarily expressed through the Sympathetic and Parasympathetic Nervous Systems. Put crudely, the Sympathetic Nervous System

(SNS) stimulates 'fight or flight' when faced with perceived threats, preparing us for action, like diverting blood from the gut to the muscles, faster breathing and raised heartbeat. Conversely, the Parasympathetic Nervous System (PNS) prepares the body to 'rest and digest', to chill out: more blood for the guts, slower breathing.

Past studies have examined the relationship between various stressors, including parental conflict, and either the SNS or the PNS, separately. The new study looked at the joint effect on both systems at the same time.

It found that children developed externalizing behaviour in response to parental conflict if both PNS and SNS were simultaneously switched on. If the 'fight-or-flight' responses were going full blast with the 'rest-and-digest' doing the same, the child was likely to be reported by both parents and teachers as being prone to externalizing.

This was because the SNS system seems to override the PNS, the child becoming angry, even chaotically furious, and getting involved in fights with his parents, who then start using extreme measures to control the child, up to and including hitting him. The pattern now established, the child takes it to school, with teachers reporting him to be more liable to fight, disrupt classes and be prone to inattention.

Equally, if the child's response to parental conflict is for both systems to shut down, he is unable to produce adequate emotional responses, reacting neither actively nor chilled. Instead, he will go into a state of passive vigilance, leaving him wide open to the nasty scenes and unable to express his distress or anger. Such children are more prone to delinquency and inattention at home and at school.

In contrast, when children react by either one or the other system going into action, they are much less likely to externalize.

They seem to be protected by active coping responses, like becoming healthily distressed or keeping a safe distance but trying to calm everyone down.

Given the huge body of evidence showing that, from before birth onwards, these electro-chemical systems are heavily influenced by nurture, it is highly probable that prior experiences (and not genes) establish the basic pattern with which they respond to later exposure to parental conflict. Put simply, if you row a lot with your partner in front of the children, how they differentially react will depend on their earlier experiences.

Hence, if things went swimmingly for all your children early on (during the first six years), the chances are that they will cope much better when you row. The main implication is to take particular care to reassure those of your offspring who may have fared less well early on.

In Mary's case, it is likely that she has had a mixture of nervous system responses established, which are activated only at home. There, it would seem, both systems are liable to be switched on, creating a fight reaction, her aggression and impatience. More subtly, her active attempts to pacify and protect the family may have been a version of this. On top of that, at night her furious feelings turned into a terror of being abandoned.

That LB seems to have doused her reactivity could be because it did indeed reset her thermostat to some extent. After the LB, it may be that she had only one system activated at a time, not both simultaneously, producing a healthier reaction. Allied to the resetting of Ella's own balance, mother and daughter could have been set off on a different, more benign trajectory.

Alas, thermostats can be changed. When Ella came back to me with a further report, the change had been for the worse in Mary's case.

One year later: Ella's progress report

For about two months after the LB, the improvement was maintained in Mary's patience, stability of mood and capacity to recover if she became distressed. During this time, her sisters and father found it hard to accept that she had changed, tending to stigmatize her as badly behaved and difficult even if she was not. Despite this, the progress was sustained.

Two initial events set Mary back. The first was when she went away for a weekend with her father. Whilst she enjoyed it, the trouble was she felt upset to be separated from Ella and unsettled by the disruption.

The second event was Ella taking Maddy away for a weekend LB. Originally, Ella had felt she must offer LB to her other daughters because they complained that Mary was getting special treatment. Ella took Gemma off to Paris for a weekend, and when she got back, Mary rapidly combusted back into her former state of anxiety and anger. Finally, a few weeks after that, Ella took Maddy off for her weekend. Following that, they were pretty much back to square one, in terms of Mary's calmness.

All was far from lost. Mary's fear of being snatched was considerably less and remained so. Whilst the idea still worries her and emerges from time to time, it is less of a problem. What is more, Ella feels that following the LB, they 'definitely have a better relationship. The *Snoopy* book still gets chosen as a bedtime read. It bonds us that she knows I find it funny, we enjoy it together, and it is a memento of the LB weekend.'

But two fundamental facts of their family life are still disturbing Mary. The most important is that Tim and Ella continue to be at each other's throats. Mary finds this as distressing as ever. Ella comments that 'The key to Mary's upsets is my fraught relationship with Tim. However successful what you do when away with the LB, it's going to be undermined if the context that created the problem in the first place stays the same when you return to it.'

The other is that, regardless of her behaviour, the *dramatis personae* in her family seem determined to cast Mary as irritating, jumpy and troublesome. All of us are assigned scripts in our family drama. As a scriptwriter or director, Ella seems unable to persuade her older daughters or her husband to recast Mary in a more positive light. Their tendency to see her as a problem turns into a self-fulfilling prophecy. As Ella says, 'I am trying to protect her from what's unfair, but her siblings and father are attacking her [as had Ella in the past]. It's an everyday event, and it's having a cumulative effect on who she is.'

Of these difficulties, the first is the greatest. Tim and Ella are seeing a new couple therapist, and Tim remains resolutely reluctant to face the fact that his childhood is affecting the way he is reacting. Of course, Ella is also bringing baggage from her own childhood. Having been one of six siblings in a rivalrous, tempestuous family, she is desperate to protect Mary from the same experience. But she also becomes highly emotional, something that Mary may be imitating to some extent.

For all these problems, there is still a good chance they will ultimately be able to understand how their histories are affecting the kind of family they are creating. If Tim and Ella can get onto a happier footing as a couple, Ella believes everything will follow from that, and I suspect she is right. If that happens, it is not too late for Mary to rediscover the calmness she found on the LB weekend.

STORY 19

An awayday – single father
Self-loathing, tantrums, overeating:
Sheila, aged 11

Sheila is 11, her older sister is 14. Her father, Brian, is divorced from their mother, Diana. Brian contacted me because he hoped to do LB with his daughter, feeling it unlikely he would be able to persuade Sheila's mother to do it.

Sheila's problems

Sheila has very low self-esteem, amounting to self-loathing. She has tantrums when being controlled by her mother or sister. No amount of close contact seems to be enough, it never fills her up. She escapes from the awfulness of life through watching *Horrible Histories* TV programmes and playing a computer game. These are restricted to half an hour a day when she is at home. She eats compulsively, but she is not yet overweight, just definitely chubby. Her mother is similar in this respect.

She makes long telephone calls to Brian rather than doing her homework. He enjoys them to a certain extent and is not that bothered about her homework. Sheila is very bright and passed the exam to the local grammar school, but she describes this achievement as 'the deodorizing airspray to hide the stink that is me'.

She hates games but, when taken on a walk, she ends up liking the fresh air and, Brian surmises, liking being alone with her mother. She frequently shares her big bed. He thinks she gets 'a really, really good cuddle' from her mother most nights.

She spends little time with Brian, her older sister having taken a stand against visiting him. Sheila wants to be with her sister, who, sadly does not want her around and is verbally cruel to her. Her sister is busy striking out, ploughing her own furrow, like doing a job two days a week in a local shop. She does not want to be held back by this person whom she criticizes for being overweight. Says Brian, 'That's really sad, because they do love each other.'

Their mother, Diana, is very impatient with Sheila because she 'goes off on one' so frequently. The slightest contretemps results in shouting by both of them, which is then, unfairly in Brian's view, punished by removal of some privilege, like computer time. Although Brian and Diana had gone to parenting classes together, she still believes in punishment, which Brian does not.

Diana keeps healthy food in the house and never shames Sheila about her eating. However, just as her mother did, Sheila gets up early in the morning and consumes vast numbers of slices of white bread, before then having breakfast.

The LB

Brian planned the LB two weeks ahead, after he had said, 'I would love to go up to London with you, spending time doing what you want.' They did not give it a name.

Sheila opted for a visit to Harrods food halls, a trip to Madame Tussauds, a visit to a shop to buy her Mum's Christmas present, and lunch at her favourite restaurant. They would travel up and down by train. She would be in charge of what and when they ate and drank.

They had a harmonious time together, achieving all the goals she had set. However, there was an unfortunate break from the LB. Says Brian, 'What I regret is that I had to have a 1½-hour detour to my flat to meet a plumber. That interfered with the process. She had to sit there waiting while I dealt with that; it was something that was not for her or controlled by her.'

The effect of the LB

Brian reports that 'although she enjoyed the day, it made no fundamental difference to her problems. I don't think it was for an extended enough period of time. It was better than nothing, but it didn't get her into a zone where she really relaxed and felt safe and in control. She was still thinking, "won't it be awful when I get back home".'

Following the day, Sheila did seek more contact with him, having lengthy daily phone calls.

During them, she conveyed her tension and unhappiness and described crying on her way to school. It is a highly competitive one, leading Brian to the conclusion that she is feeling under too much pressure there.

Sheila reported to her mother, who conveyed it to Brian, that the day had made her more keenly aware of his age, 50. Says Brian, 'This was complete with complaints about my antiquity and then followed by feelings of guilt at the complaint.'

However, subsequently, he reports: 'We did spend an afternoon together after school making ravioli with her own creation for the filling, a lovely event.'

Brian's hopes for the future

He would like Sheila's mother to do LB but, because of their awkward relationship, realizes he is not the best person to suggest the plan. Nonetheless, he feels she may agree to try it. There is a problem about what they would do with the older daughter whilst Sheila was away with her mother. The older daughter will not come and stay with him. I suggested that perhaps he could go and stay with her while her mother was away, or that she could stay with a friend. He agreed that both of these were possibilities.

Why the LB may not have worked

Despite his benign intentions, Brian was unable to follow several of the basic LB rules. Although he did give Sheila the feeling of control, they did not agree a name for the experience, there were no mementos, and, above all, the already brief period was interrupted by the detour to meet with the plumber.

Perhaps most fundamentally, since Brian does not live with his daughter, just doing the LB was never going to be enough. A significant part of Sheila's problems are in her relationship with her mother and sister. On returning home, she was back to square one: nothing there had been changed by the LB. If the LB is done with a parent the child lives with, an important component of its efficacy is changes in the way the parent relates to the child afterwards. Inevitably, that was lacking in this case.

STORY 20

One night away
A dyspraxic, self-hating and meltdown-prone identical twin: Tina, aged 7

Tina, 7, has an identical twin, Hester, and a younger brother. Her mother, Pam, is thoughtful and diligent and has cared for the children full-time at home since birth, with a supportive husband.

Tina's problems

Both girls have been diagnosed as having Special Needs, suffering from an inability to make delicate, fine movements and to plan, a disorder known as dyspraxia. However, their psychology differs. Tina is nervous, becoming furiously angry, with temper tantrums. Pam says, 'She goes from nought to seventy in arousal in no time at all, panics, hasn't got a good self-regulatory mechanism.'

Tina also has low self-esteem. She is very sensitive and emotional. Pam says that she internalizes everything (blames herself if things go wrong) and then has a massive meltdown. When you speak to her about it afterwards, she says, 'I am a terrible person', 'I hate myself'.

Pam also says that Tina has 'quite a lot of autistic traits, although none of the teachers or other professionals or I think she is actually diagnosable as autistic, or on that spectrum.' Of both twins she says, 'They are above average intelligence, they speak well, did so before they were 1, that's an area of strength.'

Pam believes that most of Tina's bad behaviour and distress results from her dyspraxia: 'She has to work hard just to get through everyday stuff, like tying her shoelaces. A lot of her nervousness, anger and meltdowns can be attributed to having to deal with constant frustration on a day-to-day basis.'

Hester, her genetically identical sister, also has the dyspraxic difficulties yet copes with them differently. Pam describes her as 'much more determined, so she has higher self-esteem. She is not as sensitive. If she has a big meltdown, it's somebody else's fault. I think she may have the dyspraxia to a lesser extent, but it's hard to gauge that because she also tries a lot harder.'

The fact that these genetic identikits are so different is something of a mystery to Pam. She is tremendously energetic in seeking practical help for her girls, yet when it comes to their psychology, little seems to help. She finds it hard to identify noticeable patterns that explain Tina's changes in mood, whether internal to her or external, like family rows or other triggers.

She was attracted to the idea of LB because her mother did something very like it when she was small, and Pam still recalls the experience fondly.

Planning the LB

For practical reasons, they could only do one night away, so the LB period was two full days and one night. Tina gave it a name, 'Our Special Tina Time Away'. There was quite a lot of build-up, which caused a few problems with Hester, although Pam committed to doing the same for her. Pam told Tina: 'You can do whatever you like.' In advance, she did not want to do very much; the main thing was swimming, so they booked into a hotel with a pool.

The LB

They set off on the Saturday morning to go by train. There were all sorts of things Tina wanted which she would not normally be permitted, like a magazine to read on the train and sweets.

Once at the hotel, they spent a lot of time swimming, becoming 'wrinkled like prunes'. Says Pam, 'She can swim and likes doing it, but most of the time she just wanted to be on my back and playing, not what we would normally do.'

In the evening, Tina wanted to watch *You've Been Framed* on TV. She had specified that she wanted to go for a three-course meal in the restaurant. In doing so, she ordered 'far too much and wasn't that hungry, so I got them to take part of the dinner up to the room so we could have it in bed on this room-service platter.'

They slept in the same bed and went down for breakfast in the morning. Tina was in a tremendous hurry to go swimming again. Pam believes she did have a feeling of being in control and that Tina 'found the telling her I loved her a bit strange at first, but she was fine with that. She's quite a huggy, cuddly girl compared to Hester.'

The Top-Ups

The problem was that Pam's husband does not get home until after the girls go to bed, so the plan was to do the Top-Ups at weekends. Called Mummy Time, Pam would do it for both girls, each getting to go with her on their own, like for a coffee and to buy a book in a shop. They did manage to do it for a bit, but it has now fallen by the wayside.

The impact of the LB experience

Pam noticed no change in Tina's self-esteem and anxiety levels, nor any other discernible effect on her behaviour.

However, she feels the experience did mean a lot to Tina. She says, 'Tina quite often mentions the weekend: it's something she looks back on fondly, it was a highlight in her life.' What is more, she feels that 'it did improve our relationship, it made her feel special. We probably need to do it again, thinking of our relationship now. It affected the way Tina felt about the way I feel about her. That has been sustained. But that had no effect on her behaviour because I think most of that is beyond her control and mine.'

Possible reasons why the LB did not alter Tina

Two things may explain the lack of effect of the LB. Partly, it could be that Tina's dyspraxia was untouched by it and that the frustration she feels as a result of the disorder continues to trigger her self-hatred and anger. It is possible that the difference between the twins in how they react to their dyspraxia, and the extent of the deficit, was caused by differences during the pregnancy. Interestingly, there can be a considerable difference in the womb experiences of twins (whether identical or not). For example, one twin often manages to take up larger amounts of space in the womb or to kick the other.

The second possibility, however, is that Pam has found herself no longer believing that she can have much effect on how the twins turn out, considering them as being beyond her control. As she explains, 'They have a neurological issue and their emotional states do not seem to be influenced by how people react to them. I feel a bit powerless. The extent of their dyspraxia on any given day varies. They can wake up fine on one day, then the next a learnt skill has gone, "Why can't I do this, I could do it yesterday?"' It is possible that something of this despair and helplessness affected how Pam did the LB.

She was not lacking in basic commitment to the principle, saying, 'My mother did something similar with me. My little sister had just been born. It was a weekend away where I was allowed to do what I wanted. I still remember that now. I do think these things have an impact, and I don't think the LB was a waste of time at all. I will do the same with Hester.'

Of Tina, she says, 'I wish I could put my finger on what makes her tick. She has calm phases, and she was in one at the time of the LB. For quite a long time she will be calm, and then for another equal period she will be completely crazy. We're in a crazy patch at the moment. She hates everyone and everything.' When I asked Pam for more detail regarding Tina's state before and after the LB, she realized it had had a greater effect than she first suggested. She had chosen that weekend because Tina had just started at a new school at that time. Although she was quite calm then, she was feeling down about herself because she felt she lacked friends, thinking she was rubbish. Pam said, 'It's true that after the weekend she self-criticized a little bit less.'

POSTSCRIPT

There is abundant scientific evidence that parents who believe they can affect their children's behaviour are in better spirits than those who do not. Even more important, parents and teachers who believe they can have an effect actually are more likely to have one. But, most important of all, if children see themselves as mutable, they are better able to change. For example, if they are given four lessons teaching them that they are capable of increasing their ability to do maths, they subsequently do improve, compared with children given no lessons. The more convinced they were that their maths ability was immutable before the lessons, the greater the change that occurs in their subsequent performance.

The important implication is that, even if your child does seem to have an inborn or unchangeable trait, it is best to keep on hoping that things can change. Whilst it is sensible not to have unrealistic expectations of what a brief intervention like Love Bombing can achieve, if you go into it with enthusiasm and optimism then that is the attitude most likely to bring success.

FURTHER READING

Relevant self-help books

Biddulph, S. (1999). *The Secret of Happy Children*. London: Thorsons.

Jackson, D. (2003). *Three in a Bed: The Benefits of Sleeping with Your Baby*. London: Bloomsbury.

Jepsen, J. (2006). *Born Too Early: Hidden Handicaps of Premature Children*. London: Karnac.

Kohn, A. (2007). *Unconditional Parenting: Moving from Rewards and Punishments to Love and Reason*. New York: Astria Books.

Piontelli, A. (2002). *Twins: From Fetus to Child*. London: Routledge.

Clinical and scientific sources

Gerhardt, S. (2004). *Why Love Matters: How Affection Shapes a Baby's Brain*. Hove: Brunner-Routledge.

Gerhardt, S. (2010). *The Selfish Society: How We All Forgot to Love One Another and Made Money Instead*. London: Simon & Schuster.

James, O. W. (2002). *They F*** You Up: How To Survive Family Life* (revised edition, 2007). London: Bloomsbury.

James, O. W. (2010). *How Not To F*** Them Up*. London: Vermilion.

Laing, R. D. (1971). *The Politics of the Family*. London: Penguin.

Miller, A. (1991). *Banished Knowledge*. London: Virago.

Weich, M. G., et al. (2006). Outcomes of prolonged parent–child embrace therapy among 102 children with behavioural disorders. *Complementary Therapies in Clinical Practice, 12*: 3–12.

Winnicott, D. W. (1954). Withdrawal and regression. In: *Through Paediatrics to Psycho-Analysis* (pp. 255–261). London: Karnac, 1992.

www.lovebombing.info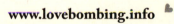